MICHAEL
JACKSON
1958-2009
A CELEBRATION

MICHAEL JACKSON

1958-2009
A CELEBRATION

GRAHAM BETTS

Reynolds & Hearn Ltd
London

First published in 2009 by
Reynolds & Hearn Ltd
61a Priory Road
Kew Gardens
Richmond
Surrey TW9 3DH

A CIP catalogue record for this book
is available from the British Library.

ISBN 978 1 904674 10 8

Designed by James King

Printed and bound in Malta by Progress Press Ltd

COVER: Michael Jackson performs in Los Angeles at the closing
concert of the Bad Tour, 27 January 1989. Greg Allen/Retna/Corbis

ACKNOWLEDGEMENTS

Many thanks to Michael Heatley for the introduction and to Richard Reynolds for the opportunity of writing this book – I only wish it had been under different circumstances. Thanks also to Sharon Davis for her encouragement over many years, much of which has been spent discussing and dissecting Motown! I am also indebted to numerous authors and journalists who have covered Michael Jackson's career over the years and whose work proved useful in the writing of this book, in particular J Randy Taraborrelli, Berry Gordy, Nelson George, Margo Jefferson, Walter Tetnikoff and Michael Jackson himself. An extra special thanks to my family, Caroline, Jo and Steven – we can get back to normal now!

CONTENTS

INTRODUCTION

The initial call to 911 gave no indication that one of the biggest stories of the millennium was about to break. It began with the simple statement that an ambulance was needed as soon as possible to be sent to Los Angeles, California, 90077. That, the operator who took the call was able to ascertain, was Carolwood Drive.

Over the next few minutes the caller became more and more frantic as he described how a 50-year-old man needed help, was not breathing and that a doctor who was in attendance was performing CPR to no avail. Seemingly, neither the caller nor the operator was in any hurry to identify the 50-year-old who needed assistance.

An ambulance arrived inside four minutes, with the medics from the Los Angeles Fire Department also attempting CPR before transferring the man to Ronald Reagan UCLA Medical Center. A little over an hour after he arrived at UCLA, it was announced that Michael Joseph Jackson was dead.

Even before the official announcement issued at 2.26pm, rumours and stories were circulating around the globe, thanks to the internet. It was thought that the first outlet was a celebrity internet site, who had been alerted by one of the medics who had attended the address at Carolwood Drive. By the time the major newspapers and television news carried the announcement, most of Michael Jackson's fans were already aware that there was a major problem – CNN, Fox News and their ilk merely confirmed the worst fears.

Michael Jackson's death and the aftermath has been conducted in much the same way as Michael Jackson's life

– in the full and constant glare of the media. There have been rumour and counter rumour, stories, more allegations and media investigations into almost every aspect of his life and his career. Michael Jackson never got any peace whilst he was alive, so why should it be any different now he is dead?

The death of a celebrity invokes all manner of emotions, ranging from the gushing eulogies issued by fans and friends through to the barbed comments from those with another agenda to pursue. Michael Jackson's death has been no different, so it is in the middle ground that we find perhaps the most meaningful impressions and analysis of what Michael achieved and what he meant.

The bare facts are impressive – more than 750 million records sold worldwide, 13 Grammy awards, including eight in one year (still a record), a total of six BRIT awards, and two stars on the Hollywood Walk of Fame for his contribution to recording and radio.

Yet there was always more to this talented but complex man than mere record sales. Briefly married to Lisa Marie Presley, Michael Jackson shared many similarities with her equally famous father, Elvis Presley. Both were acclaimed at some time in their careers as the King of Pop, both sold more records than any of their counterparts, yet both had troubled lives away from the stage and recording studio. Elvis Presley died from a heart attack brought about by prescription drug abuse, whilst initial reports of Michael's death seem to attribute much the same cause. Both were about to embark on major tours that they perhaps didn't want to undertake, but pressure from management (in Elvis's case) and creditors (in Michael's) seemed to dictate. Elvis's last meaningful record prior to

his death had been 'The Wonder Of You', a number one
hit in the UK seven years before his death. In Michael's
case his last number one had been 'Blood On The Dance
Floor', a good twelve years before he died. Yet Michael's
star, which had been burning for nearly 40 years, was
seemingly about to rise again; the announcement that
he was to perform at the O2 Arena in London in July
had been met with unrivalled ticket demand and what
was originally envisaged as a small number of live dates
on a farewell tour grew into a virtual residency at the
former white elephant on the banks of the River Thames.
Ultimately a million tickets would be sold for the 50 dates,
proof that Michael Jackson didn't need a current hit record
to sell a venue, especially where his vociferous and loyal
British fans were concerned. Once the King of Pop,
always the King of Pop.

How much pressure the impending shows placed on
Michael Jackson we will look at later, but it was known
that privately even Michael was apprehensive about what
he had signed himself up for. Fifty dates would have
been a daunting schedule for a man of 25 – for a man of
Michael's age, with expectations always so high (has there
been a better live performer in any musical genre over the
last 25 years?) and the frailties of his health there were
many who felt that 50 dates was a task too far. The events
of 25 June 2009 convinced those who had questioned
the wisdom of the number of dates that they were right
to doubt all along. For much of the rest of the world, the
death of Michael Jackson brought about an outpouring
of grief and emotion not seen since the death of Princess
Diana some twelve years previously.

Every generation will have their own memories of
Michael Jackson. For some it will be the fresh faced boy

who burst onto the scene with his brothers as the latest act to roll off the Motown conveyor belt - the music may have been formulaic, but the performances were anything but. For others it will be the sheer energy of such tracks as 'Rock With You' and 'Don't Stop 'Til You Get Enough' – still rightly ranked among the best dance music ever produced. Others will recall the moonwalk on the Motown television special, the routines he came up with for 'Billie Jean', 'Beat It' and 'Thriller' – indicative of a man who had all the right moves and a worthy successor to the likes of Fred Astaire.

Whichever generation you belong to and whichever memory of Michael you most cherish, there is no doubt that his untimely death brings to an end one of the most compelling careers in popular music. From humble beginnings in Gary, Indiana to lavish extravagance in Neverland, California is a long journey – this book is a celebration of that journey and the career of Michael Jackson along the way.

GRAHAM BETTS, JULY 2009

CHAPTER ONE
FROM STEELTOWN
TO MOTOWN

T he 50 or so years between the end of the Civil War and America's entry into World War I saw unrivalled growth in the United States. Britain may have been the first country to embrace the industrial revolution, but America's emergence as a former British colony struggling to find its feet into the economic powerhouse of the world was little short of remarkable.

Most of the wealth was created in the northern States. With New York in general and Wall Street in particular providing the bulk of the funding, new industries sprung up in a small enclave of states, thus ensuring that an even smaller group of individuals grew ever richer.

One such individual was Elbert Henry Gary. After graduating first in his class at the Union College of Law, Elbert practised in Chicago and also kept an office in Wheaton. There was plenty of work to be found in both cities, with Elbert specialising in attorney work for the numerous railroad companies based in Chicago. The work must have been lucrative too, for Elbert later linked with his uncle Jesse Wheaton to found the Gary-Wheaton Bank, a bank that survived until it was merged with Bank One during the 1990s!

Elbert Gary continued his highly successful law career for some 25 years, serving as a judge for two terms in DuPage County from 1884 to 1892. It was while serving as a judge that Elbert Gary first came across the burgeoning steel industry. The actual case he heard has been lost in the mists of time, but the complexities of the business together with the mind-boggling sums of money that could be made were enough to attract his interest. Six years after finishing his second term as a judge, Elbert Gary became installed as the president of the Federal Steel Corporation in Chicago. Federal was already a big player in the steel industry in Chicago – the fact that they made barbed wire would ensure a steady flow of income for years to come.

Yet as big as Federal Steel Corporation was in 1898, it wasn't big enough for the ambitious Elbert Gary. He re-located the business to New York in 1900 and over the next 12 months made a number of powerful and influential friends around Wall Street, friends who would enable him to move onto the next stage in his plan. Key among them were financier and banker JP Morgan, industrialist and businessman Andrew Carnegie and fellow businessman Charles Schwab. Schwab had founded the Bethlehem Steel Corporation and had managed by the turn of the century to turn it into the second largest steel manufacturer in the United States. Carnegie had similarly founded the Carnegie Steel Company in Pittsburgh, another major player in the market. Encouraged by JP Morgan, the three steel magnates realised that – as big as they were singularly – collectively they would be untouchable. Thus on 25 February 1901, JP Morgan and Elbert Gary merged Federal Steel with Bethlehem Steel and Carnegie Steel, together with a number of other smaller companies, to form the United States Steel Corporation, at a cost of $492 million. The new company was capitalised at $1.4 billion, making it the first billion dollar corporation in the world.

The new company, which quickly used the shortened name US Steel, became the biggest steel manufacturer in the United States overnight, controlling almost two thirds of the country's steel production. Yet despite its size, US Steel still had a number of problems to contend with, not least the huge amount of debt it saddled itself with on its start-up, mostly due to the fact that Andrew Carnegie had not been convinced enough to accept shares in the new venture and instead insisted in being paid in gold bonds for Carnegie Steel.

Elbert H Gary would serve as president and chairman of the board of the new company from its inception until his death in August 1927, at the age of 82. While Elbert Gary made his home in New York, he looked elsewhere for sites to develop the new company. In 1906 US Steel selected a site in Indiana for their new plant, also building a new town in which to house the workers. Named Gary in honour of the chairman, the town would become synonymous with the steel industry for more than 70 years. By the end of the century, Gary was home to over 100,000 inhabitants, making it the fifth largest city in the state. US Steel's fortunes also rose and rose and during the Second World War, when production of some 30 million tons of steel was required to aid the war effort. More than 340,000 workers were employed by the company nationwide.

One such worker who would eventually graduate to Gary was Joseph Walter Jackson. Born in Fountain Hill in Arkansas, to Samuel Jackson and Crystal Lee King in 1929, Joe was the oldest of the eventual four children born to the couple before they separated in 1941. Joe went with his father to Oakland in California, remaining on the West Coast until he turned 18 and graduated from high school, at which point he turned his back on a boxing career and moved east to Chicago to live nearer to his mother. Living in the same vicinity was Kattie B Screws, the daughter of Martha Mattie Upshaw and Prince Albert Screws. In 1934 Albert decided to change his surname to Scruse, with the four year old Kattie also changing her name and becoming Katherine Scruse.

Always a man with an eye for the ladies, Joe met and

married another woman before he came across Katherine. This marriage was brief and eventually annulled, with Joe subsequently courting Katherine and eventually marrying on 5 November 1949, a date that was no doubt hastily arranged as Katherine was already pregnant. The first child Maureen Reilette (today better known as Rebbie) would enter the world on 29 May 1950. The newlywed couple made their home in a two-room house costing $800 in Gary, where Joe found work as a crane operator at the US Steel plant.

For the first half of the decade, Joe and Katherine no doubt presented a picture of domestic bliss – Joe working full time at the steel mill and Katherine staying at home to look after their growing family. After Rebbie's birth in 1950, the Jacksons were blessed with their first son, Sigmund Esco (better known as Jackie), being born on 4 May 1951. Eighteen months later, on 15 October 1953, Toriano Adaryll 'Tito' came into the world. A little more than a year later, on 11 December 1954, came Jermaine LaJuane.

It was at this point that Joe began to pursue visions of a career well away from the sweat and toil of the steel mill. Along with one of his brothers, Luther, Joe formed a group known as The Falcons, with Joe playing guitar. The group was soon able to get a number of local live dates around the town. Live work was a means to an end for Joe; each date would enable The Falcons to develop a fan base and before long record company scouts would come looking to see what all the fuss what about before offering a lucrative recording contract.

Despite the dreams, reality turned out to be completely different. While The Falcons did indeed establish something of a following in Gary, it was never enough to attract the scouts out of New York or Los Angeles.

Even those companies based in Detroit showed little or no interest in The Falcons and eventually what work they had began to dry up. This caused Joe more of a problem than any other member of the group, for his family was still growing. On 29 May 1956 Joe and Katherine welcomed their second daughter La Toya Yvonne and ten months later, on 12 March 1957, Katherine gave birth to twins Marlon David and Brandon. Sadly Brandon died at birth, but less than eighteen months later a fifth son, Michael Joseph, was born on 29 August 1958.

By the time Michael was born, Joe had abandoned all thoughts of pursuing a music career and had gone to the steel company, cap in hand, to ask for his old job back again. The dream may have come to an end for Joe inside two years, but the experiences he went through would later prove to be extremely beneficial, both for him and his growing boys.

Growing up in the Jackson household wasn't easy, however. Joe had to work long and hard hours at the steel mill in order to provide for his large family, with Rebbie and Jackie helping their mother in bringing up the younger children. Day times in the household were invariably filled with laughter, the kind of laughter and fun only young children can have and enjoy. By the time their father came home, the Jackson siblings learned that it was better to be seen but not heard, for Joe had a fearsome temper and was also a strict disciplinarian. The children all learned at an early age that they did not do anything that Joe would disapprove of, did not answer back, and accepted everything their father said as Gospel.

Like most boys, the Jackson brothers were inquisitive souls who would often open doors and drawers which they knew they weren't allowed to while their father was

around. One such door revealed Joe's guitar, which Tito
in particular took interest in. Over the next few months,
Tito would play with the guitar while Joe was at work,
careful to return it to its exact resting place before father
got home. And for months the deception worked, with Tito
becoming especially competent on the instrument. Jackie
and Jermaine also took turns in playing, but eventually
the strain of three young boys playing the instrument
was bound to lead to trouble – one day a string broke and
the boys were forced to return the guitar to the cupboard
and hope their father wouldn't notice! There was no
chance Joe wouldn't notice such a thing, and there was a
fearsome scene when the broken string was discovered.
Extremely angry at the boys' deception, Joe at least gave
them a chance to redeem themselves; if the string had
been broken by them trying to learn how to play the guitar
properly, then the boys had an opportunity to show what
they had learned. Fortunately for them, they all proved
more than capable, and Joe was impressed enough to
suggest the three form themselves into a group.

Drafting in friends Reynaud Jones and Milford Hite
on guitar and drums respectively, the Jackson Brothers
were formed in 1964, with Joe believing there was enough
potential in the group to go part-time at the steel company
and part-time as manager and chauffeur for the group.
Local fairs and fetes proved the ideal location for the
group's early dates, performing as Ripple & The Waves
and The Jackson Brothers, with their reputation around
the town eventually leading to bigger and better dates.
The success that the three eldest brothers were enjoying
had both Marlon and Michael keen to lend their support,
and by the following year both were added to the backing
group playing tambourine and congas. Another brother,

Steven Randall (known as Randy) was born on 29 October 1961, but was plainly too young to perform with this incarnation of the group).

While Michael was the youngest member of the group and kept mainly in the background for the best part of a year, his personality and talent soon began to make their presence felt. Eventually he was allowed to show his dancing skills at a talent contest held at Roosevelt High School, where Jackie was a pupil. 'We had to wear white shirts and short trousers ...and got the biggest applause. When I went to my seat, my grandfather and mother were crying. They said "We can't believe how beautiful you sound."'

Thanks to Michael, the Jackson Brothers won the competition – further adding to their profile around the town. Shirley Cartman, who taught Tito at junior high school, suggested switching from Reynaud Jones and Milford Hite to Johnny Jackson on drums and Ronnie Rancifer on keyboards, with Tito switching to lead guitar and Jermaine becoming bass guitarist. Jermaine had been the group's original lead singer, but Michael eventually took over the role as if born to play it. Shirley Cartman also suggested a name change to The Jackson Five, the name under which the group would eventually become world famous.

It was one thing to win a school talent contest, quite another to go out on the road and perform professionally. Doing so would require more than talent; conviction, practice and discipline were needed, and Joe was able to provide all three in abundance. The sternest of task masters, Joe seemed to reserve his harshest criticism for Michael. As the newly-installed lead of the group, it would invariably be Michael that the audience would fix their stare upon. Thus Joe worked Michael almost to the point of collapse, ensuring all of the dance moves were spot on, all the lyrics memorised to perfection and all the cues met with ease. Not content with merely pointing out mistakes, Joe would often resort to both physical and emotional pressure to make sure his point got home. Many years later Michael would claim he had been the victim of physical and emotional abuse from his father, with Marlon once stating that 'Joe held Michael upside down by one leg and pummelled him over and over again with his hand, hitting him on his back and buttocks.'

The abuse was not only restricted to rehearsal time for the group. On another occasion, after he had repeatedly told his children not to leave doors or windows open at night, Joe decided to prove his point by climbing into Michael's bedroom wearing a fright mask and shouting and screaming at the sleeping boy. For many years after, Michael held a real fear of being kidnapped from his bedroom!

While the abuse had a profound and lasting effect on Michael, it did at least ensure the group was as professional as could be while out on the professional circuit. Word of their abilities went beyond Gary, with the Jackson Five getting dates as far afield as Chicago in Illinois and right across Indiana. One such show saw them on the same bill as the legendary R&B act Sam & Dave, who arranged for the group to enter the Amateur Night competition at the famous Apollo Theatre in New York's Harlem. The group duly entered and won the contest on 13 August 1967 – also impressing Gladys Knight, who was in the audience that night. Already with two major names on their case, it appeared only a matter of time before the Jackson Five landed a recording contract. Yet it would take Gladys a considerable time to get anyone to listen to her at Motown, while Sam and Dave felt that Stax Records, where they were on the roster, was not the right label for the group.

Eventually the group's reputation around Gary was enough to attract the attention of Gordon Keith, a producer at the appropriately named Steeltown Record Company. Founded in 1966 by Ben Brown, Steeltown Records would have a shortlived and unsuccessful history (it closed its doors in 1972), but the very fact they were the first label to show any concrete interest in the Jackson Five has ensured their lasting reputation. While big money was already being made by the likes of Motown Records in Detroit, Steeltown Records was an extremely small company, effectively a one man operation. Gordon Keith scraped together what money he had to put the group into the studio, with recording sessions beginning in October 1967 on what would eventually become the group's first single, 'Big Boy'. The boys provided their own musical accompaniment to Michael's lead vocals on a song written by Ed Silver, with 'You've Changed' being recorded at much the same time for inclusion on the B-side. The Jackson Five would eventually record some eleven tracks for Steeltown, with Keith expecting to issue an album somewhere along the way if either 'Big Boy' or 'We Don't Have To Be Over 21 (To Fall In Love)', the planned second single, proved to be a success.

'Big Boy' was eventually released in January 1968 and, as expected, did become a local hit in Gary, selling well around the town. The boys were also extremely excited to hear their single played on local radio, with the family gathering around a set in order to hear what the DJ thought of the record and the boys. In truth, there wasn't too much to get excited about; 'Big Boy' was fairly typical of the

Motown derivatives that were being released in towns
and cities all across the United States, the groups and
singers often as anonymous and nondescript as the labels
that released them. That did not diminish the feeling of
immense pride in the Jackson household, however, with
Michael later stating that the whole family jumped for joy
and had a family hug when 'Big Boy' got its first play.
'We felt we had arrived' was his simple comment.

'Big Boy' would go on to sell some 10,000 copies
locally, making it the biggest hit to emerge on the
Steeltown label and possibly the biggest single to have
been produced in Gary. Yet those figures were nowhere
near enough to make even a small dent in the all-important
charts; no appearance on the Billboard Hot 100, the
Cashbox chart, not even the R&B chart. And 10,000
copies was not going to make The Jackson Five rich; the
limited contract Gordon Keith had signed the boys to
ensured them three cents a record, and that would have to
be split five ways *after* Joe had taken his management cut!

Sales of the second single 'We Don't Have To Be Over
21 (To Fall In Love)' were even smaller (although this
single, together with 'Some Girls Want Me For Their
Love' re-appeared on the Dynamo label in 1971 when
Jackson mania was at its height), giving Gordon Keith
something of a dilemma to ponder over – was it worth
releasing an album if the group had little more than a local
fan base to call upon? In the end it didn't really matter,
for the work the Jackson Five had put in earlier, performing
at the Apollo Theatre and having the likes of Sam & Dave
and Gladys Knight champion their cause, had attracted
the interest of Motown Records and had ensured that
at the very least they would get an audition in Detroit.
Once Motown became involved, there was no way that

Gordon Keith could compete and he reluctantly handed over control of the group after being recompensed by Motown. It is worth mentioning that Gordon Keith made little or no money out of the Jackson Five – after they had signed with Motown, Keith kept his Steeltown Records label operative for a couple of years and then virtually disappeared from sight. The tracks recorded during 1968 were long thought lost until the mid 1990s, when a family friend found a box of tapes in the pantry of his parent's kitchen. Perhaps realising their importance, Ben Brown had the tapes re-mastered and issued as an album on the Inverted Records label, even going so far as to produce a video for the 'Big Boy' track. The album would eventually become something of a staple on countless budget record labels around the world and continues to turn up to this day, the ultimate ownership of the tracks being long lost in the mists of time. Gordon Keith himself finally got around to cashing in when he put a number of artefacts of the Steeltown era up for auction in 2009 – included in the sale were mint condition copies of the two singles. Keith stated at the time 'I could use the money – I got these guys off the ground and I didn't truly get real money for it.' The death of Michael Jackson has surely added to the value of those records.

It was while the Jackson Five were on the road promoting 'Big Boy' that they began to attract wider interest. Bobby Taylor, lead singer of the multi-racial R&B group The Vancouvers, is largely credited (at least these days) with being the first to spot the boys potential and ensure that everyone within Motown was aware of the group. It wasn't until later in 1968 that The Vancouvers own career would take off, with the group scoring three hits that year in 'Does Your Mama Know About Me',

'I Am Your Man' and 'Melinda', which would certainly account for the reason why Motown changed the name of the act that supposedly discovered the boys. And Bobby Taylor wasn't the only one taking more than a passing interest. Gladys Knight & The Pips were an established act before they signed with Motown and knew talent when they saw it. Gladys was reportedly knocked out by the five brothers she had seen at the Apollo and couldn't wait to tell Berry Gordy and Norman Whitfield all about them the next time she was in Detroit. In fact, Gladys made two separate attempts to get Motown interested in the Jackson Five, singing their praises to her manager at ITM Taylor Cox. It was Bobby Taylor's persistence however that finally got them through the door at Motown, a performance at Chicago's High Chaparral Club convincing him that Motown would be missing out if they didn't offer the group at least an audition.

Accompanied by Joe, the five brothers travelled to Detroit on 22 July and spent the night on the floor of Bobby Taylor's apartment in the city. There were a few last minute panics, for the following day the boys were to undertake the biggest event of their lives, albeit in front of very few people! Berry Gordy himself wasn't going to be there, but Motown, and in particular one senior executive, Suzanne De Passe, had ensured that Gordy would get to hear about it since they were going to film the audition so he could watch it in his own time in Los Angeles. His comment on the video was that 'Michael danced like James Brown, sounded like Jackie Wilson and performed a Smokey Robinson song, and I later said to Smokey, you know, he nailed you on it!'

Although 'Big Boy' had been a regional hit (and if Berry Gordy was in tune with what was happening in the music world, he would have been familiar with the song), the Jackson Five chose to perform the James Brown hit 'I Got The Feelin'', a song that had topped the R&B charts and made the top ten of the Billboard Hot 100 (exactly where the Jackson Five wanted to be!). While the vocal and instrumental performances were passable, what made the audition stand out was the sheer exuberance of Michael: his dancing, singing and smiling were as fresh and clear on film as they were in real life. It was this aspect of the performance, perhaps more than any other, that would finally convince Berry Gordy the Jackson Five were worth taking a chance on.

It should be fully understood that Berry Gordy signing the Jackson Five was never a foregone conclusion, despite the success of the audition. To begin with, Berry had already experienced signing child singers. He had one of the best in Stevie Wonder – although, by this time, Stevie was an 18-year-old and a child star no longer. But it was the memory of the problems Gordy had had with Stevie, or more importantly the authorities – who were concerned that Stevie would spend too much time trying to be a pop star and not enough time doing his school work – that planted the seeds of doubt in Berry's mind. There was also the matter of the existing contract with Steeltown Records, which wasn't due to expire until March 1969. By then Berry might well have discovered somebody else, or gone off the idea all together. Fortunately, Suzanne De Passe, no doubt aided by Gladys Knight and Bobby Taylor, kept up the pressure and when Berry finally got to see the boys in the flesh, he was as convinced as the rest of his company that this was indeed a special group. He instructed his legal department to begin negotiations with Steeltown to buy the Jackson Five out of their contract. A financial settlement was finally reached between the two companies.

The contract that the Jackson Five finally signed with Motown Records was better than the contract they had had with Steeltown, but only just – a 6% royalty rate against 90% of the wholesale price, which was apparently the standard Motown rate. Once divided five ways, it meant each member got less than half a cent a copy sold on singles and two cents per album. There would also be $12.50 for each song recorded, but this would only be paid if the record was released. It must have seemed a fortune to the Jackson Five, but compared with the rest of the industry, where 8% was the norm, it was a paltry amount. Despite this, it was a contract that the Jackson Five were happy to sign, inking their names to the one year contract on 26 July 1968.

After a performance at Berry Gordy's Detroit mansion for all of Motown's staffers, the boys went into the Hitsville Studios (as the Motown studios were named) to record their Motown debut. In charge of the early sessions was Bobby Taylor, who worked the group through some 30 tracks, including a series of contemporary hits and standards such as Sly & The Family Stone's 'Stand' and a stunning version of Smokey Robinson's 'Who's Lovin' You' (which eventually turned up as the B-side to their debut single 'I Want You Back'). Listening to the tapes, Berry Gordy was impressed. But if the Jackson Five were to really break through, there was much additional work to be done. He decided to scrap the Taylor-produced sessions and move the group to Los Angeles, where he was spending more and more of his time, and really work on grooming the Jacksons and their act.

Although the Jackson Five were already an experienced act by the time they joined Motown, Berry Gordy and

Suzanne De Passe put together a completely different package to present to the public. To begin with, the publicity department changed the story of their discovery by Motown, so that the credit would go to Diana Ross. According to the publicity handout, Miss Ross had travelled to Gary to attend a benefit concert for Mayor Richard Hatcher, at which the Jackson Five performed. Suitably impressed by their performance, Miss Ross told Berry Gordy that he just had to sign them up. This attachment to Diana Ross was to be carried through the group's debut album and beyond, and while Diana Ross and the Jackson Five, in particular Michael, developed a close bond over the years, it wrote Bobby Taylor and Gladys Knight out of the picture.

Many of the early Motown acts had received grooming from the label, including instructions from the Artist Development department on what to say in interviews, how to walk properly, what to eat in restaurants and so on. These sometimes basic instructions were designed to ensure Motown was projected in the best possible light at every opportunity. If an African American singer from the ghettos of Detroit was to perform in front of a member of the Royal Family at the London Palladium, then he or she had to be coached to do the right thing. The Artist Development department was in its heyday while Motown was headquartered in Detroit. The eventual switch to Los Angeles saw its importance diminish, but it still had one last important job to undertake: to turn the five Jackson brothers from Gary, Indiana into a group that the whole world would embrace. Berry Gordy handed over this task to executive Suzanne De Passe.

A talent co-ordinator at Cheetah, Suzanne De Passe developed a friendship with Cindy Birdsong, the eventual

replacement for Florence Ballard in The Supremes,
meeting up whenever the pair were in the same town.
At one such meet, Suzanne had booked a limousine
because 'in those days it was still hard to get a taxi if
you were black. Cindy asked if she could ride with us,
and Berry – being the chauvinist he is – apparently
thought I was a go-go dancer.' Despite the confusion over
their first meeting, Berry thought enough of Suzanne
to mark her down as an executive to watch for in the
future. When, a few months later, Suzanne rang Berry to
complain about some problems she was having booking
Motown acts and how the talent co-ordination department
needed something of an overhaul, Berry offered her the
job. Initially appointed as creative assistant to Berry
himself and based in Detroit, Suzanne quickly rose
through the ranks and was eventually one of the first ten
staffers at the label's new headquarters in Los Angeles. 'I
can tell you when I took over I had absolutely no idea how
a deal was struck, no idea how the pie was split up for
royalties, no idea what happened to a record after the tape
leaves the studio and heads towards the marketplace.'

Suzanne De Passe's lack of knowledge of the record
side of the business did not stop her from making
numerous contributions to the grooming of the Jackson
Five. While the rehearsal sessions in Los Angeles were
invariably run by Joe Jackson, it was Suzanne's suggestion
that the group drop the James Brown material. If the group
were to appeal to middle-class America, then more pop-
orientated material was going to be needed. Suzanne also
worked on the boys' wardrobe, ditching the jeans and
T-shirts in preference for Day-Glo outfits that certainly
made them stand out in a crowd!

While Suzanne De Passe was undertaking her crash

course in band management, Berry Gordy decided it was time he got more involved in finding the right material for the group to record. While the bulk of Motown's biggest hits had come from the pens of Brian Holland, Lamont Dozier and Eddie Holland ('I Can't Help Myself', 'Reach Out I'll Be There', 'Where Did Our Love Go', 'Baby Love', 'You Can't Hurry Love' and many more), H-D-H had effectively gone on strike in an attempt to leave the label in pursuit for a bigger slice of the royalty pie. There were other songwriters and teams within Motown, but none in Berry's view had the credentials necessary to come up with the right kind of material. So, just as he had done with Diana Ross's material before her departure from The Supremes, Berry decided to take control. He assembled a new team of Deke Richards, Alphonse (Fonce) Mizell and Freddie Perren, and put them to work. The first song the team looked at was one they had already written with Gladys Knight & Pips in mind: 'I Wanna Be Free'. The song underwent significant amendments. The lyrics were changed, the key lowered and other alterations made along the way as The Corporation, as the song writing team were dubbed (no doubt to ensure the writers and producers did not become as famous or popular as Holland-Dozier-Holland), worked up the song to become 'I Want You Back', with instructions from Berry to give the end result a Frankie Lymon feel. The song is about a lover deciding he has been too hasty in ditching his partner and deciding 'I want you back'; the fact that the lead singer wasn't even a teenager appeared not to matter!

Berry Gordy's didn't only suggest changes in the studio. The initial press kits sent out to promote The Jackson 5 (another change Berry made, switching the spelt out

'Five' to the number, which would later lend itself for marketing purposes much better) made the group younger than they were – Michael for instance, was now a cute eight-year-old rather than the eleven-year-old he actually was! The previously unrelated Johnny Jackson now became a cousin to the group, as did fellow backing group member Ronnie Rancifer. Aside from suddenly becoming honorary family members, there was little else for Johnny Jackson and Rancifer to do, for Motown used professional studio musicians in Los Angeles to provide the musical accompaniment for their recordings, including various members of The Crusaders.

Preparations for the group's launch into the world continued throughout 1969. In between rehearsals Joe, Tito, Jermaine and Jackie lived with Berry while Marlon and Michael stayed with Diana Ross in her California home, but work was the major priority, getting the group's background story straight and honing their dance routines. The newly-named Jackson 5 were finally ready to be unveiled to the public on 11 August 1969 with a performance at The Daisy, a club in Beverly Hills in Los Angeles. At the end of the month came their first television appearance, performing a cover of The Isley Brothers' 'It's Your Thing' at the Miss Black America pageant at Madison Square Gardens. Then, two months later, 'I Want You Back' was finally released as a single on 7 October. To back up the release, the Jackson 5 were scheduled to perform at The Hollywood Palace where they performed their single and covers of Sly & The Family Stone's 'Sing A Simple Song', The Delfonics' 'Can You Remember' and James Brown's 'There Was A Time'.

Few labels had enjoyed the kind of sustained success that Motown had enjoyed during the 1960s. And even

fewer had enjoyed success with such an identifiable sound
as the Motown Sound, the 'sound of Young America'
as Berry liked to describe it. Yet Motown virtually re-
invented itself with the Jackson 5's debut single 'I Want
You Back'. Described by many as the perfect pop song,
it was an infectious slice of bubblegum soul, instantly
catchy on the airwaves and as sure fire a smash as anything
Motown had released in the previous few years.

The public obviously thought so too, buying enough
copies to ensure the record entered the chart by the middle
of November and begin its ascent up the US charts. It hit
number one on 31 January 1970 (in the UK it fell one
place short, kept off the top by Lee Marvin's 'Wand'rin
Star' backed with Clint Eastwood's 'I Talk To The Trees'),
by which time the group were also enjoying a presence
on the album chart with their debut long player *Diana
Ross Presents The Jackson 5*. The album would contain
only one single release in 'I Want You Back' and one
other composition from The Corporation in 'Nobody'.
The rest of the album was made up with tracks that had
been produced in Detroit by Bobby Taylor, including
'Who's Lovin' You' (this version is still considered the
definitive version of the Smokey Robinson song, carried
almost entirely by Michael's exquisite vocals) and covers
of 'Standing In The Shadows Of Love', 'My Cherie
Amour', 'Chained' and '(I Know) I'm Losing You' from
the Motown catalogue and 'Stand' (Sly & The Family
Stone) and 'Can You Remember' (The Delfonics) and
'Zip-A-Dee-Doo-Dah' from elsewhere. While the rest
of the album was a radical departure from the single
that preceded it, it did not stop the album selling in vast
quantities and making the Top Five of the Billboard Top
200. In so doing the Jackson 5 instantly became one of the

most successful of all Motown groups, for Motown was not renowned for its success on the album charts during the 1960s, and Marvin Gaye and Stevie Wonder's regular appearances with their blockbusters were still a few years away. The album also enjoyed considerable success in the UK, making a very respectable #16 on the Music Week charts.

In less than four years the Jackson 5 had gone from playing school fetes to topping the Billboard Hot 100, a remarkable journey that promised well for the future. Yet the success came at something of a price, one which would eventually have to paid by Berry Gordy.

CHAPTER TWO

AS SIMPLE AS ABC

Whem the Jackson Five, as they were then, first started out on the road to stardom it was very much a family effort. Joe was their manager and chauffeur, ferrying them around the country from one date to the next. Mother Katherine also played her part, sitting up in the evening sewing and repairing their outfits. Even the other Jackson siblings joined in, with Rebbie and La Toya taking over the tambourine duties that had previously been the preserve of Michael and Marlon. In time, so would Randy and, even further down the line, the last of the Jackson children Janet Damita Jo (who had been born on 16 May 1966) would become involved.

The Jackson 5's initial success did at least benefit the family, who left Gary behind and bought a two-storey house at 1616 Queens Road in Los Angeles. A year later they bought a bigger property, a mansion they dubbed Hayvenhurst. But apart from setting up a new home, there was little for Joe to do as Berry Gordy was masterminding and commanding the group's assault on the charts. And Katherine's sewing machine fell idle as the group were given new outfits on a regular basis for television appearances and live dates around the country. While the boys were enjoying their new-found fame and slowly growing fortune, Joe was simmering with discontent.

Berry probably wouldn't have cared even if he had noticed, for he was too busy supervising The Corporation's efforts to come up with more material akin to 'I Want You Back'. While 'ABC' sounds as though The Corporation were probably writing by numbers, the arithmetic certainly added up. The single was as catchy and punchy as its predecessor. And the team worked hard to ensure that the follow-up album was equally as strong and as laden with potential hits as possible, with 'The Love You Save' being earmarked as a potential single too.

In all, The Corporation came up with four new tracks for the *ABC* album: the title track, the aforementioned 'The Love You Save', 'One More Chance' and 'I Found That Girl'. The cover versions, like the debut album, came from a wide variety of sources. Motown's own catalogue provided '(Come 'Round Here) I'm The One You Need' (originally by The Miracles), 'Don't Know Why I Love You' (Stevie Wonder), the aptly titled 'The Young Folks' (Diana Ross & The Supremes) and 'Never Had A Dream Come True' (Stevie Wonder again). From outside Motown came 'LaLa Means I Love You' (The Delfonics again) and 'I'll Bet You' (Funkadelic).

'ABC' was released as a single in March 1970, followed two months later by the album of the same name. The single took barely six weeks to top the charts in the US, dislodging The Beatles' 'Let It Be' in the process and remaining there for two weeks. Its success fuelled demand for the album, which would eventually make it #4 on the Billboard charts, one place better than its predecessor and certainly worthy of an album that was crafted rather than compiled the way *Diana Ross Presents* had been. In the UK the album made #22, while the single was another Top Ten success, peaking at #8.

The success of the first two singles and albums gave Motown something they had never previously had – an act that could appeal across the board. Parents loved the fresh faced boys – especially the youngest Michael, who sang seemingly innocent songs and danced exceptionally well. Their children liked them too and wanted to be like them. And not just the traditional R&B market; here was an act that appealed across the colour lines, for white audiences were as enthralled with the Jackson 5 as their black counterparts. This success would eventually open up avenues that Berry Gordy had previously only dreamed about, and which he and Suzanne De Passe were quick to exploit.

While 'ABC' was on top of the charts, The Jackson 5 were sent out on the road, headlining for the first time at the Convention Center in Philadelphia. They played to full and enthusiastic audiences wherever they went, setting a new attendance record at the Great Western Forum in July. By then the group were also enjoying their third consecutive number one smash as 'The Love You Save' also knocked The Beatles with 'The Long And Winding Road' off the top again! In the UK, 'The Love You Save' went one better than its predecessor and hit #7, the group's third Top Ten hit in a row. By September, Motown were proud to report that the group, already firmly established in the minds of the public as the latest teen sensation, had sold over a million records inside nine months. Earlier, Motown had been claiming that each of the three debut singles had sold over a million copies, so no doubt Joe would be checking the royalty statement with extra vigilance!

In October came another headlining tour, kicking off in Boston at the Boston Garden. Meanwhile, back in Los Angeles, Berry Gordy had decided to pull the group's planned fourth single 'Mama's Pearl', which had been written by The Corporation, in favour of a departure from the norm. 'I'll Be There' had been written by Bob West and re-worked considerably by producer Willie Hutch; the version recorded by the Jackson 5 was a stunning ballad that really showed Michael's vocal abilities. The earlier, up-tempo numbers could have been sung by almost any competent singer; 'I'll Be There' demanded a great singer, which Michael was well on his way to proving.

So, having already established one record by becoming the first act to top the US charts with their first three records, The Jackson 5 stretched the record to four when 'I'll Be There' dethroned Neil Diamond's 'Cracklin' Rosie' on 17 October 1970. It would go on to become the biggest Jackson 5 single of all, topping the charts for five weeks and selling more than four million copies in the process. In the UK it had to be content with resting at #4 on the Music Week chart, still a very healthy performance.

With the single still hot, Motown quickly released a third Jackson 5 album, imaginatively entitled *Third Album*. There weren't many acts that could expect to release as many as three albums inside one year (a figure that was to be stretched to four by December), but Berry Gordy was keen to exploit the Jackson 5's new found fame for all it was worth. Yet *Third Album* would go on to become the group's biggest album of the year, topping the R&B charts and making #4 on the Billboard Top 200 (it did even better on the Cashbox chart, where it made it all the way to number one). Led by the smash hit 'I'll Be There', the album followed the well-trodden path of their earlier efforts: two Motown covers in 'Oh How Happy' and 'The Love I Saw In You Was Just A Mirage', new material such as 'I'll Be There', 'Mama's Pearl', 'Goin' Back To Indiana' and 'Can I See You In The Morning' and another cover version in 'Bridge Over Troubled Water', a song that had been the bestselling single of the year for Simon & Garfunkel. Despite the success the album enjoyed in America, *Third Album* missed the charts altogether in the UK.

In December came the fourth Jackson 5 album of the year. Over the years Motown had regularly got their stable of artists to record traditional Christmas material, with the likes of The Temptations, The Supremes, The Four Tops and Stevie Wonder covering much the same material on their respective albums. The Jackson 5 were no different, with everything from 'Frosty The Snowman', 'Rudolph The Red-Nosed Reindeer', 'Santa Claus Is Comin' To Town' and 'I Saw Mommy Kissing Santa Claus' being given the Jackson 5 teen soul treatment. The album proved especially popular in the US, where it topped the Billboard Christmas Albums chart (for some reason, Billboard did not put Christmas albums on the main album chart), but a single release of 'Santa Claus Is Comin' To Town' backed with 'Someday At Christmas' and 'Christmas Won't Be The Same This Year' capitalised on the British fascination for Christmas material by hitting #43 on the charts.

As 1970 eventually came to a close and the boys settled down for their first Christmas in their new home in Los Angeles, they could reflect on a stunning and successful year. Four number one singles, four chart albums and worldwide popularity had ensured the Jackson 5 had arrived as a major force in the music world. No doubt there were extra special presents given by Berry Gordy and the other members of The Corporation, for thanks to the Jackson 5 they had sold more records than almost any other song-writing team during the year. The pressure would be on to match those achievements in 1971, both for the group and The Corporation.

Berry Gordy could be forgiven for thinking that the early contributions he had made to The Corporation had established a blueprint for future material, and there is evidence that the songs the remaining members of the team came up with were nearly as strong as those first three singles. Yet Gordy was already finding other projects to occupy his time. The main reason for moving Motown's headquarters to Los Angeles had been to try and break into other areas of the entertainment industry, including film and television. His vision was to turn his protégé and love interest Diana Ross, now on her way to solo stardom, into the biggest female performer in the world, and to do this he needed the right film vehicle for her to star in. Gordy had also left much of the day-to-day activity of the Jackson 5 in the capable hands of Suzanne De Passe, but she too had prioritised other projects, effectively leaving Joe back in charge of his sons.

Other problems were soon to surface. In Detroit, the talented writers and performers had all gravitated to Motown because it was the biggest record company in the city (by a series of takeovers engineered by Berry Gordy it was on its way to becoming the only record label in the city). There they had all played their part in putting Motown on the map, and been appropriately rewarded. In Los Angeles however, there was an abundance of rival record companies to contend with, most of whom cast envious eyes at the staffers at Motown and wondered if they could be prised away. The bottom line was that for the right money, anyone could be bought and moved on. So eventually Fonce Mizell would leave and turn up at Blue Note, where he wrote and produced a number of classic cuts for Donald Byrd. He would be followed by Freddie Perren, who would link up with Kenny St Lewis and produce a series of Jackson 5 influenced tracks for another family outfit The Sylvers – and then with another former Motown staffer in Dino Fekaris write classics such as 'Reunited' for Peaches & Herb and 'I Will Survive' for Gloria Gaynor.

While the Jackson 5 were still hot, the pending departures were not a problem. Motown had seen the departure of Holland-Dozier-Holland and not only survived but prospered. And besides, that was the whole point in forming The Corporation: it enabled an individual member to be replaced effortlessly. And for much of 1971, the Jackson 5 remained hot.

Having earlier rejected 'Mama's Pearl' in favour of 'I'll Be There' in October, Berry now decided to release the track as a single in January 1971. At first it sailed its way through the chart, quickly hitting number two as Jackson-mania showed little sign of diminishing. To support the single the group made a triumphant return to Gary, performing a benefit concert for Mayor Richard Hatcher's re-election campaign. In honour of the group's exploits the previous year, the city renamed Jackson Street to Jackson 5 Boulevard for the day!

'Mama's Pearl' was unable to dislodge the incumbent number one single 'One Bad Apple' by the Osmonds. This was especially galling for Berry Gordy, for he had been offered the song by writer George Jackson and rejected it for the Jackson 5 as being too juvenile! But 'Mama's Pearl' did sell another million copies in the US and make it to #25 in the UK, so the hope was that the single not making to the top of the chart was merely a temporary blip.

In fact, the Jackson 5 were never to return to the top of the chart, at least in the US, although there were still plenty more hits to come. To follow-up the up-tempo 'Mama's Pearl', Motown returned to ballads for 'Never Can Say Goodbye', released as a single in April 1971. Written by Clifton Davis, 'Never Can Say Goodbye' was another chance for Michael to shine and his performance was as complete as it could be. The single hit number two in the US, this time kept off the top by Three Dog Night's 'Joy To The World'. In the UK the single stalled at #33, the third successive single to miss out on making the Top Ten.

Later the same month came the accompanying album *Maybe Tomorrow*. Because of the success of 'I'll Be There', most of the material comprised ballads, although there was nothing else on the album with the same kind of instant appeal as that stellar single. The success of 'Never Can Say Goodbye' and subsequently the title track, which hit #20 in August (writer Deke Richards originally composed the song with Sammy Davis Jr in mind) was enough to propel the album to #11 on the Billboard charts. While not as successful as their three debut albums, it ensured the Jackson 5's continued presence in the charts.

In July the five boys taped their first television special, *Goin' Back To Indiana*, which was due to air in September. Also featuring comedians Bill Cosby and Tommy Smothers, fellow singers Bobby Darin and Diana Ross, and an assortment of American football and baseball players, Motown wasted little opportunity in putting together a soundtrack album for the group's next release. Featuring live versions of their hits that had been recorded in their May performance in Gary, *Goin' Back To Indiana* appeared in the shops after the special had aired on ABC. It made the Top Twenty too, peaking at #16 in November.

The ABC special wasn't the only television activity during the year, for after the special ABC and Motown reached agreement for a cartoon series that would begin airing in September 1971. A specially recorded medley of the group's four biggest hits, 'I Want You Back', 'ABC', 'The Love You Save' and 'Mama's Pearl' served as the theme to the Saturday morning series, with pictures of the

group members morphing into cartoons setting the scene.
During the course of the series, the group would undertake
a wide variety of tasks in order to drum up publicity,
including farm work and performing for the President.
The tasks were usually set up by the band's manager
Berry Gordy, with assorted other celebrities popping up
somewhere along the way.

Animated in London and Barcelona, the series may
have been all about the Jackson 5, but they didn't actually
appear in it! Michael's voice was provided by Donald
Fullilove, Edmund Sylvers did Marlon (a real irony, given
the later success that the Sylvers family was to enjoy as
something of a clone of the Jackson 5), Joel Cooper was
Jermaine, Mike Martinez was Tito and Craig Grandy
did for Jackie. Even Berry Gordy's voice was provided
by someone else, in this case Paul Frees. Stars such as
Diana Ross did at least provide their own voices. Another
interesting aspect of the cartoon was the placement of a
number of exotic pets that Michael was supposed to have,
including pet mice Ray and Charles and a snake named
Rosey. The series would run from 11 September 1971
until 1 September 1973, with a total of 17 episodes being
made for the first series and six for the second. The show
was repeated on ABC during the 1984-85 season, when
Michael Jackson mania was at its height.

As a promotional tool for the real Jackson 5, the cartoon
series enabled the group's growing catalogue to get a
regular airing, with two songs being featured in each
episode. In the second series, songs from Michael's solo
album came to the fore. The success of the series, together
with continued recording success, led to an abundance
of licensing and merchandising for the Jackson 5, with
stickers, sew on patches, colouring books and other items

aimed at maintaining the popularity of the group in the coming months.

Although the Jackson 5 had enjoyed considerable success during the first two years of their career with Motown, Berry Gordy had in mind bigger and better things for Michael, convincing him that a parallel solo career would aid both him and the group. He was keen to assure the rest of the family that this wasn't the first stage in separating Michael from the group – the group's name was not going to change to Michael Jackson and the Jackson Four, as had been the earlier case with Diana Ross and The Supremes. Besides, Berry Gordy had selected a number of songs for inclusion on the album that just didn't work in a group environment, including a remake of 'Rockin' Robin', originally a #2 hit for Bobby Day in 1958. Gordy also had in mind putting Michael virtually head to head with another family – Donny Osmond was about to release his debut solo album at much the same time, and having lost out in the battle with 'One Bad Apple', Berry had revenge in mind!

Released in December 1971 and promoted with an appearance on Diana Ross' television special that month, 'Got To Be There' returned at least one member of the Jackson family to the Top Ten. A #4 hit on Billboard's pop and R&B chart, it did even better on the Cashbox listings, where it made it to number one. The single was another international success too, peaking at #5 in the UK. The album duly appeared on 24 January 1972, and would make it to #14 in the States and #37 in the UK. Both sides of the Atlantic went with 'Rockin' Robin' as the second single, with the decision vindicated when it hit #2 pop and R&B in the US (kept off the top by Roberta Flack's 'First Time Ever I Saw Your Face') and #3 in the UK.

Motown in America went with 'I Wanna Be Where You Are' as the third single, which hit #16 in the US. The song itself, written by Leon Ware and T-Boy Ross (Diana's brother) would go on to become one of the most popular by this particular team, with covers by artists ranging from Marvin Gaye to The Fugees appearing over the years. In the UK, Motown's licensor EMI chose the Bill Withers song 'Ain't No Sunshine' as the third release from the album. While Bill's original had been a smash in the US, where it hit #3 a year previously, the single had missed out in the chart altogether in the UK (it finally became a hit in May 2009 after one of the entrants in the X Factor covered it), giving EMI the opportunity to market it as virtually a new song. The ploy worked, for 'Ain't No Sunshine' hit #8 and became the UK's definitive version of the song.

With solo success to go with the group's continued fortunes, 1971 had been as hectic a year as its predecessor, with the expectations of maintaining the hits and the revenue rolling into Motown only set to increase in the years to come. Despite this success, Michael was already beginning to feel pressured. Now he had two careers to worry about. While he continued to portray an image of a fresh-faced bright youngster to fans and media alike, privately Michael was not entirely content. When not working, which was seldom, he spent much of his time with Diana Ross and bemoaned the fact that he was missing out on the usual things that children got to do. He could not go to the zoo or Disneyland or the cinema or any of the things ordinary teenagers got to do because he was not ordinary. Fame had brought luxuries, the like of which Michael had only dreamed off as a child growing up in Gary. But fame came at a price – and that price was his childhood.

There was little time for excursions anyway, for Michael was kept busy in the studio recording both group and solo material for release during 1972, as well as having to keep up with his school work. 'I would do my schooling which was three hours with a tutor and right after that I would go to the recording studio and record, and I'd record for hours and hours until it's time to go to sleep. And I remember going to the record studio and there was a park across the street and I'd see all the children and I would cry because it would make me sad that I would have to work instead.' Even touring was becoming something of a chore. 'We were getting ready to go to South America and everything was packed up and in the car ready to go and I hid and I was crying because I really did not want to go. I wanted to play – I did not want to go.' Crying seemed to be the only way Michael could express his displeasure at the pressures being placed upon him. Even the little 'fun' time he had brought him sadness. 'There were times when I had great times with my brothers, pillow fights and things, but I used to always cry from loneliness.'

Yet work was what Michael and his brothers had to concentrate on. A greatest hits package was released in January, offering the casual buyer the chance to get all of the group's hits on one album – it hit #12 in the US and #26 in the UK, further helped by the single 'Sugar Daddy' making #10 pop and #3 R&B. Meanwhile, the group were busy working on their fifth studio album, *Lookin' Through The Windows*, and cracks were beginning to appear right across the board. To begin with, Michael's voice was about to break, turning him from a boy soprano to a tenor. Both Michael and the rest of the group felt that the material they were being asked to record was still firmly entrenched in the bubblegum soul that had proved so successful a couple of years earlier. Yet Motown wasn't prepared to listen to any of the arguments for change that the boys and their father put forward: Motown in general, and Berry Gordy in particular, knew best.

The album would eventually hit #7 in the US, with the singles 'Little Bitty Pretty One' (a cover of Thurston Harris' 1957 hit, which had previously been covered by Bobby Day and Frankie Lymon, among others, and done in a similar style to 'Rockin' Robin') hitting #13 and the title track also hitting #13, helping push sales throughout the year. In the UK, the Clifton Davis written 'Lookin' Through The Windows' became the group's first Top Ten hit in 18 months as it hit #9. As a follow-up, EMI chose 'Doctor My Eyes', a cover of Jackson Browne's US Top Ten hit from 1972. As the original had missed out in the UK altogether, EMI was sure they could replicate the success of 'Ain't No Sunshine' and were rewarded when 'Doctor My Eyes' also hit #9.

In September 1972 came the second solo album from Michael. In 1971 the film *Willard*, about a killer rat, had been an international success, and in 1972 came plans for a sequel titled *Ben*. Written by Don Black and Walter Scharf, the song was originally intended for Donny Osmond to record, but at the time The Osmonds were on tour and Donny was unavailable. Don Black therefore suggested that the song might be ideal for Michael; his version made it to #1 in the US, where it spent a week, #7 in the UK and earned nominations for a Golden Globe for Best Song (which it won) and an Academy Award for Best Original Song (it lost out to 'The Morning After' from *The Poseidon Adventure*). The title track was easily the best song on what was a ragbag collection of covers and new material, with none of the other singles issued troubling the Top 40 on either side of the Atlantic.

As 1972 came to a close, the gap between Motown and the Jackson family was growing into a chasm. Both Michael as a solo artist and his brothers as a group were dismayed by the material they were being asked to record by the label. Joe would have frequent heated arguments with Berry Gordy on his family's behalf, but Berry was showing little sign of bending his 'Motown knows best' attitude. Berry was certainly not interested in hearing any of the material the brothers had written and therefore had no intention of allowing them to record their own compositions. Thus the two albums issued during 1973 came to reflect the simmering disagreement between the family and Motown; Michael's *Music & Me* pictured Michael with an acoustic guitar on the cover, even though he did not perform musically on the album at all, while the Jackson 5's *Skywriter* features the boys looking solemn on the cover. There had been virtual warfare in the studio during the recording sessions, with Jermaine (who was also enjoying a solo career) and Michael objecting to the inclusion of 'Touch', a song originally recorded by The Supremes and concerning satisfying a woman in bed. Yet while the Jackson family vented their anger at the Motown hierarchy, there were still moments to lighten the mood, as producer Hal Davis later revealed. 'Sometimes recording with those boys was just so much fun. We'd do the serious part, the recording of the music and vocals and then sit around listening back to what we'd achieved. And woe betide me if I fell asleep during the sessions; I'd often wake up to find the boys had written on my face or were trying to set my shoelaces on fire. Boy, we had some fun back then!'

Skywriter would be the least successful Jackson 5 album up to that point, making only #44 in the US and missing altogether in the UK (and *Music & Me* fared no better, barely hitting #92). Yet there were some high points, with the title track attracting some attention from the growing disco movement (and a UK #25 hit) and 'Hallelujah Day' making #28 pop and #10 R&B in their homeland and #20 in the UK. A third single, 'Boogie Man' missed out on chart honours almost everywhere, further convincing the boys that their future would be better served if they had a greater say in the material they were recording. While Motown may have been reluctant to give the Jacksons their head, others within the company were being freed from the reins. Stevie Wonder and Marvin Gaye were now making heavy inroads into the album charts. Even more galling, The Commodores, who had signed for Motown in 1971 and toured extensively with the Jackson 5 as their opening act during their first few years with the label, made it quite plain right from the start that they intended writing and performing their own material. So if it was good enough for The Commodores, why not the Jackson 5?

About the only concession Motown allowed was sharing the lead vocal duties around for what proved to be the final two albums the group recorded for the label. *G.I.T. Get It Together* therefore features almost as many lead vocals from Jermaine as it did Michael, and Tito came to the fore on 'Mama I Gotta Brand New Thing (Don't Say No)'. The title track, just about the last thing The Corporation wrote for the group before effectively disbanding, became a modest Top 30 hit, with the album barely making the charts at all, peaking at #100. The project was saved, however, by the release of the last track on the album, 'Dancing Machine', another nod towards disco, that would briefly return the group to the upper echelons of the chart, making #2 pop and #1 R&B (yet missed out altogether in the UK!) and was kept off the top by Ray Stevens 'The Streak'. A hasty re-packaging job ensued, with *Dancing Machine* being fleshed out with leftover tracks. Despite the hurried assembly of the album, it returned the group to the Top 20, peaking at #16.

Although both Michael and the Jackson 5 would release material during 1975, their time at Motown was at an end. Joe had been negotiating with Berry Gordy for months but found neither Berry nor Motown were particularly interested in giving the boys what they really wanted – control of their own destiny. So there could be no agreement on allowing the boys to write and record their own material, either collectively or individually. This, even more than the financial considerations, was the deal breaker for the Jacksons. The brothers, with one notable exception, therefore instructed Joe to shop around for a new deal.

Joe eventually got into conversations with Ron Alexenburg and Steve Popovich, two executives from Columbia. Joe convinced Ron and Steve that his boys were worth big money, and while the executives were sold on the idea of signing the group, they knew that the amount of money being asked for would require formal agreement higher up on Black Rock, the famous New York headquarters of the major record company. The man who would eventually rubber stamp the deal, Walter Yetnikoff, was not entirely convinced. Like most of the industry, he was aware of the success the group and Michael had enjoyed at the start of the decade, but like most executives, he was equally aware that their popularity appeared to be on the wane; their chart positions proved that. There was little or no point in trying to find detailed sales histories either, for Motown was one of the few major record companies that was *not* a member of RIAA (the Recording Industry Association of America) and therefore did not allow anyone to inspect their books or certify sales. If the top executives at Columbia didn't know exactly how many copies a single or album had sold on Motown, the chances were that the artist who released them on Motown was equally in the dark!

It looked for a while as though the negotiations with Columbia were going to stall, with Yetnikoff later stating he was still unsure even after seeing the group perform live, but persistence on the part of Alexenburg and Popovich finally convinced him that this would be a chance worth taking. In June 1975 a press conference was held at which it was announced that the Jackson 5 would be joining the Epic label effective from 10 March 1976.

Except the Jackson 5 never got to record for Epic Records. Almost as soon as the deal was announced, Berry Gordy issued a writ alleging breach of contract and demanding $5.0 million. The group swiftly counter-sued and suddenly Motown Records, one of the most secretive labels in America, found itself having all of its dirty linen washed in public. The papers revealed that the Jackson 5 had recorded some 469 tracks for the label, of which only 174 had seen the light of day on record. Yet the Jackson 5 were responsible for all of the recording costs on the tracks; what had started out as a fee payable to each of the boys of $12.50 per track recorded (if released) had become a $500,000 bill for them as a group! The writs also revealed that the group had earned only a 2.7% royalty during their time with the label, despite having sold millions of records around the world. There was worse to come too; they had signed with Motown as the Jackson Five, but on 30 March 1972 Berry Gordy had taken out a patent on the name Jackson 5! Berry Gordy not only owned the name, he also had a bit of leverage of his own as his daughter Hazel had married Jermaine Jackson in December 1974 – while Joe, Michael, Tito, Marlon and Jackie were trying to get away from Motown, Jermaine announced that he was staying put. Joe was especially livid when he found out, stating 'My blood runs through Jermaine's veins, not Berry Gordy's.'

It was Michael who came up with a solution to the problem. The band might not be able to record as the Jackson 5, but this was going to be a new line up (Randy was to become the newest member of the group) and so a new name would seem appropriate. Berry Gordy and Motown were paid $600,000 in a settlement and The Jacksons would be the new recording artists for Epic Records. While all four Jackson members refused to record any further material for their old label, there was plenty in the can to ensure both Michael and the Jackson 5 had albums released during 1975, with *Moving Violation* being released as a group effort in July and making #36, while *Forever, Michael* barely registered at all, making #101. However, some six years later, when Michael was scoring big around the globe, Motown in the UK would dust off 'One Day In Your Life' from the album and watch with amazement as it hit #1 – the first Michael Jackson single to hit the top in the UK!

CHAPTER THREE
ENJOY YOURSELF

Aside from being one of the biggest record companies in the world, Columbia (or CBS as it was known then in the UK) had other attributes that would help break The Jacksons into bigger markets, not least the presence of a major television network. While Suzanne De Passe had had to work hard to get ABC to offer the Jackson 5 any kind of television deal, at Black Rock it was sometimes merely a case of Walter Yetnikoff asking a favour of his counterpart at CBS TV. In June 1976, therefore, CBS TV aired a four-week series entitled *The Jacksons*, featuring the new five piece line up of Michael, Jackie, Tito, Marlon and Randy together with their three sisters Rebbie, La Toya and Janet and assorted comedians and entertainers.

Meanwhile, the group readied themselves to record their debut for Epic. While Joe and the boys had visions of being let loose in the studio right from day one, the executives at CBS and Epic had other ideas. The ideas the group had about songwriting might well come good in the future, but CBS had already invested a large sum of money in the group by helping them get out of their Motown contract, and would need to get an instant return. This would not be achieved by letting the relatively inexperienced brothers have control from the outset. Rather CBS had in mind some very experienced minders.

While Berry Gordy had almost single-handedly put Detroit on the musical map with Motown Records, Kenny Gamble and Leon Huff had done much the same for Philadelphia. The pair had had a couple of false starts at running their own show, setting up Gamble and Neptune before finally launching Philadelphia International in 1971. Originally, the pair had approached Atlantic Records to fund their new operation, but Ahmet Ertegun passed on the deal as being too expensive, much as he would later do with the Jackson 5. As luck would have it, CBS Records had little or no track record in black music, a fact that was realised by then President Clive Davis, and when the opportunity came to fund a label that would make up for their own shortfall, Davis grabbed it with both hands. Over the next five years or so, Philadelphia became a serious rival to Motown, thanks to hits by the likes of The O'Jays, Harold Melvin & The Bluenotes, Billy Paul and a slew of others.

But by the time Kenny Gamble and Leon Huff were assigned to produce the Jacksons, they too had gone a little cold. It had been some two years since they had enjoyed a Top Ten hit and both had recently been embroiled in a payola scandal that had engulfed the American record industry, with Kenny Gamble being fined $2,000 for his part in the affair. There was also the fact that Philadelphia International was run on almost exactly the same lines as Motown. Recordings were invariably done in one studio (Sigma), with much the same musicians appearing on each and every release. There were teams of writers and producers who worked together; it must have seemed like a home from home to the Jacksons!

Work on what would become The Jacksons debut album for their new label commenced in late summer of 1976, with Gamble and Huff filling the roles of producers and executive producers (although production credits were also given to Gene McFadden and John Whitehead). This implied that the duo were to be responsible for almost every aspect of the recording; writing or at least selecting the material, supervising the recording and then handling post production and mixing. Yet the five Jackson brothers made it plain right from the start that the only reason they had accepted an outside production team being appointed was so that they could learn at first hand everything required to make a record. By the time recording started, Jackie was 25, Tito was 23, Marlon was 19 and Michael was 18; new member Randy had become the new 'baby' of the group at 15 but was as eager to learn as his older siblings.

It was obvious right from the start that the Jacksons were no longer the boy band that had exploded on the scene some six years earlier. They were more mature and they expected the material they were to record to reflect that maturity. This would cause some in-studio disagreements between the brothers and their producers, so Kenny and Leon asked the boys to come up with some of the material themselves; this ploy would give the team of writers Gamble and Huff had in mind an idea of the direction in which the boys wanted to go.

In the event, two Jackson compositions made it on to *The Jacksons*: 'Blues Away', which was composed by Michael, the very first published song of his career, and 'Style Of Life', which was written by Michael and Tito. Of the remaining eight songs on the album, five were written by Kenny and Leon, two by Dexter Wansel (another in-house Philly writer and producer) and the other by John Whitehead, Gene McFadden and Victor Carstephen. Despite the relatively small team responsible for the material, the album itself is a disjointed affair, indicative that Kenny and Leon just didn't know where to lead the boys.

The album was still having the finishing touches put
it when the brothers resumed their television series for
CBS in January 1977, but when it hit the bottom of the
ratings CBS cancelled its run. It was hardly the way The
Jacksons had envisaged commencing the promotion
for such an important album, and the negative publicity
the cancellation garnered must have been at least partly
responsible for the album only making #36 on the pop
charts. It did at least find favour with their traditional
fan base on the R&B charts, where it made #6. The first
single, the lively 'Enjoy Yourself', made amends, hitting
#6 pop and #2 R&B and selling more than a million
copies, while in April 1977 it hit #42 in the UK.

A month later the group arrived in Britain for their first
tour of the isles in some five years. The most prestigious
date was to be at the King's Theatre in Glasgow, a date
that coincided with Queen Elizabeth II's Silver Jubilee
celebrations, and to capitalise the UK arm of Epic put out
a second single in 'Show You The Way To Go'. While
only a minor US hit when released in that territory (it
peaked at #28) it would become the only UK number
one hit the Jacksons were to enjoy during their career,
spending a week at the top of the charts in June and
earning the group their first sales award in the UK, a silver
disc for sales of more than 250,000. This single success
helped the album into the charts too, finally making #54,
and a third and final single in 'Dreamer' was lifted in
September, hitting #22. Despite the lowly chart positions
on both sides of the Atlantic, sales were sufficient to earn
a gold disc for US sales in excess of half a million copies,
the first such award of the Jacksons' career.

While *The Jacksons* hadn't been the resounding success
that Epic had expected, it hadn't been a complete disaster,

as the gold disc adorning the wall at Hayvenhurst would confirm. Under the circumstances, therefore, Epic saw no reason to change the format for the next album *Goin' Places*. That meant going back to Philadelphia, Kenny Gamble and Leon Huff, with exactly the same writing teams being on hand to supply the material. *Goin' Places* would ultimately become the least successful of the group's Epic albums. There wasn't anything as lively as 'Enjoy Yourself' or as compelling as 'Show You The Way To Go'. If anything, Philadelphia International had reached their peak with the Jacksons on the first album, just as Motown had done with *Lookin' Through The Windows*. There were to be no pop hits extracted from the album, with 'Even Though You're Gone' becoming a UK #31 hit (something of a hangover from the popularity the group had revived during their hugely successful tour) and 'Find Me A Girl' limping in at #38 on the R&B charts. With no real hits on show, *Goin' Places* did well to make any kind of impact on the album charts, making #63 pop in the US and #45 in the UK. Only the R&B audience could be relied upon; the album topped the charts.

Michael had other things on his mind as *Goin' Places* hit the stores. In October 1977 rehearsals were due to begin for a film version of *The Wiz*. The show was ostensibly an African American update on *The Wonderful Wizard Of Oz*, with the lyrics and music being written by Charlie Smalls. The show had opened on Broadway in January 1975 with Stephanie Mills in the role of Dorothy and Hinton Battle as the Scarecrow, and had become a resounding success, going on to run for over 1,600 performances over four years. By then Motown had optioned the film rights and, together with Universal Pictures, intended turning the successful stage musical into an equally successful film.

There were several reasons given as to why *The Wiz*
was such a commercial failure, some of which were wide
of the mark and others that were spot on the nail. It did
not fail as some held because 'Blaxploitation' films had
had their day, as *The Wiz* was not aimed at the same kind
of market that had gone along to see *Shaft* or *Superfly*.
Neither did it fail because the story was too unbelievable;
it had been and continued to be a huge success on
Broadway. Yet crucial mistakes were made right at the
beginning of the film that proved insurmountable to the
cast and crew. The key mistake was in selecting Diana
Ross to play Dorothy – although, as Motown were
providing much of the funding, 'selecting' might not
be the right phrase to use. One suspects that both Berry
Gordy and Diana Ross had much to say in who got the
all-important role. Dorothy in the musical and the original
film version was a young girl - Judy Garland was 16
when she landed the part in the 1939 film version while
Stephanie Mills was 18 when she stepped on stage on
Broadway. Although conventional wisdom would have
been to give the role to Stephanie Mills (which apparently
is what Berry Gordy had in mind), Diana Ross was
desperate for the role. When Gordy turned her down on
the grounds she was too old to play Dorothy (she was
33 at the time), she went behind his back to an executive
at Universal, Rob Cohen and sold him on the idea. This
would eventually require a rewrite on the main characteristics
of Dorothy; she would now be a 24 year old schoolteacher,
which still required stretching the imagination!

Other mistakes were not as major but still contributed
to the ultimate failure of the film. The adaptation of the
script from stage to screen was cumbersome and, with one
or two exceptions, the songs weren't right to keep interest

from waning. Universal had been so excited about the prospect of the film and having Diana Ross as Dorothy that they omitted to set a budget. The final production costs hit $24 million, then a colossal amount of money which only a blockbuster success along the lines of *Star Wars* would have enabled the film to recoup.

Yet there were several bright spots. The casting of Richard Pryor as The Wiz proved that he was an exceptional actor as well as an exceptional comedian. Similarly, Michael Jackson as The Scarecrow was inspired. It may have been his first acting role but Michael threw himself into the part, spending hour upon hour watching video tapes of gazelles, cheetahs and panthers, so that he could learn how to move gracefully. Michael's performance was judged by the critics to be just about the only positive thing that could be derived from the finished result.

There was also the music, however. Initially reluctant to accept the role, Quincy Jones was apparently persuaded to do so as a favour to director Sidney Lumet. He brought in former Motown writers Nicolas Ashford and Valerie Simpson and up-and-coming R&B singer Luther Vandross to flesh out the original Charlie Smalls soundtrack. The first time the pair met in the studio, Quincy reminded Michael that they had met before, during the Jackson 5's early days at Motown, when the boys had performed at a Sammy Davis Jr party. Michael would have been about ten years of age. Michael couldn't remember the occasion in question but quickly established a rapport with Quincy, despite the disparity in their ages – Michael was still only 20 and Quincy more than twice his age at 44. Yet the pair worked some magic in the studio, most notably with 'Ease On Down The Road'.

As a standalone single 'Ease On Down The Road' might

have become a major hit, but saddled with the negative publicity surrounding the film it barely limped to #41 in the US and #45 in the UK. With domestic rentals of only $13.6 million, the film ended up showing a $10 million loss (somehow, perhaps thanks to lobbying behind the scenes, *The Wiz* ended up gaining *four* nominations for Academy Awards, in Best Art Direction, Best Costume Design, Best Cinematography and Best Original Music Score – it failed to collect any). The only positive was the working relationship established between Quincy Jones and Michael Jackson. Quincy stated that working with Michael had been one of his favourite experiences on the film, admiring Michael's obvious dedication to learning his part and his acting style, which he compared to Sammy Davis Jr. Michael himself would later claim *The Wiz* to be 'my greatest experience so far, I'll never forget that.'

For different reasons neither would Diana Ross. *The Wiz* effectively marked the end of her film career, after one too many flops. While her star had risen as high as it could, Michael's was about to go into orbit.

CHAPTER FOUR

DESTINY

As strange as it may seem now, Michael and the rest of the Jackson's story might have turned out completely differently had it not been for the continued persistence of Ron Alexenberg. One of the prime instigators behind The Jacksons' arrival at CBS, Alexenberg had to do something of a rescue operation to ensure they remained at the label in 1978. Sales of their first two albums for the company had been satisfactory but nothing more. There were other acts breaking and selling bigger quantities and as far as Walter Yetnikoff was concerned, The Jacksons had reached their peak. He instructed Alexenberg to inform Joseph that the contract between the company and the act would be allowed to lapse and not be renewed, so if they wanted to shop around for a new deal, that was fine by him. Somehow, Alexenberg managed to convince Walter Yetnikoff that there was still more to come from the Jacksons and that having had them toe the company line for the first two albums (having Gamble and Huff produce the albums), perhaps it was time to give them the chance to do what they wanted to do. Unbeknown to Joseph and his sons, therefore, Walter Yetnikoff agreed to allow one further album to be recorded – it really was make or break time for all concerned.

Almost immediately, Michael linked with Randy as something of a mini songwriting team within the larger group, with the pair eventually penning 'All Night Dancin'', 'That's What You Get For Being Polite' and 'Shake Your Body (Down To The Ground)'. The brothers collectively wrote 'Push Me Away', 'Things I Do For You', 'Bless His Soul' and the title track, while another Jackson, the unrelated Mick Jackson, was responsible for the lead track on the album, 'Blame It On The Boogie'. Written in conjunction with Dave Jackson (his brother!) and Elmar Krohn, 'Blame It On The Boogie' had been a minor German hit for its writer (Mick was born in England but later relocated to Germany) when The Jacksons first came upon the song, deciding it was exactly the kind of joyful upbeat number with which to kick-start their career (as well as being a track Epic insisted be recorded in the hope that there would be at least one hit single on the album).

Released as the first single on both sides of the Atlantic, its immediate acceptance at radio prompted Atco in the US and Atlantic in the UK to hastily revive Mick's original version. In the States the presence of two versions diluted sales demand so much that the Jacksons made only #54 on the charts, with Mick struggling to #61. The dual assault on the charts didn't seem to have much affect in the UK. The Jacksons hit the Top Ten and peaked at #8 (and earned a second silver disc award from the BPI), while Mick made it to #15. One can but wonder whether the Jacksons version might have performed better in either territory had it had the chart run to itself, but as far as the album promotion for *Destiny* was concerned, there was no confusion in the minds of record buyers; more than a million Americans bought the album, earning the group their first platinum disc as it sailed to #11 on the pop charts and #3 R&B. In the UK it had to be content with a rather more modest #33 placing, but still proved to be their most successful Epic release up to that point.

There was more to celebrate too, with 'Shake You Body

(Down To The Ground)' quickly emerging as a favourite among fans and radio alike. Its eventual release was only a matter of time, at least in the US, where it would make #7 and earn another platinum award for sales over a million copies. In the UK Epic decided to hold off release and go with 'Destiny' as the second single, a decision designed to ensure the public would have to buy the album for a little while longer if they wanted the stand out cut – 'Destiny' barely scraped the Top 40 at #39. 'Shake Your Body (Down To The Ground)' was eventually given a belated UK release in February 1979 and hit #4, earning the group another silver disc for their rapidly growing Wall of Fame.

Even now, more than 30 years since its initial release, *Destiny* remains a vital release in the Jackson story. The first album to be entirely written (with the obvious exception of 'Blame It On The Boogie'), largely performed (some of the top Los Angeles session musicians were drafted in to assist, including keyboard player Greg Phillinganes, guitarists Mike Sembello and Paul Jackson Jr and drummer Rick Marotta) and produced by the brothers, *Destiny* contained many pointers to what was about to come, especially as far as Michael was concerned. 'Blame It On The Boogie' may not have been written by Michael (at least, this Michael Jackson), but it and 'Shake Your Body' were indicative of the slick, rhythmic dance based material that would become something of a staple diet in the years to come. Similarly, the outstanding ballads, such as 'Push Me Away' and the almost autobiographical 'Bless His Soul' contained themes and images that would be revisited in time to come.

CHAPTER FIVE

WORKIN' DAY AND NIGHT

All through their career, Joseph had only ever thought about what was best for the boys collectively. Solo success for Michael and to a lesser extent Jermaine while the group was signed to Motown had been acceptable to him because it added to the demand for tickets when the group went out on the road. If Michael or any of the others wanted to do more things separately that was unacceptable; Joseph had in mind a one-for-all-and-all-for-one concept. This mentality continued in the studio. When one of the brothers wrote a song and played it to all the others for consideration, every brother and Joseph had a vote on whether it was good or bad and deserving of a place on the album. Michael's place in the hearts of the public or his earlier solo success counted for nothing as far as the Jackson family was concerned – he still had only one vote (only Joseph's single vote was allowed to carry a bit more weight than the others!).

Yet Michael in particular was beginning to feel constrained by such thinking. He did not see himself in 20 years time singing a medley of 'Got To Be There' and 'Ain't No Sunshine' on some kind of Motown Legends tour. The first strike at independence had been securing the role of The Scarecrow in *The Wiz*, something that Joseph had tried to talk him out of. When the film failed at the box office, it was proof as far as Joseph was concerned that Michael needed his brothers around him in order to achieve. Michael saw it completely differently. His performance had been one of the few positives to come out of the film, and it wasn't just him saying so, it was what most of the reviews said too. His critical success in *The Wiz*, combined with the chart success of *Shake Your Body*, convinced Michael that it was time to do another solo album, one where he would call of the shots.

Michael had little or no idea about how he wanted his debut solo album for Epic to sound, other than it mustn't sound like The Jacksons. His first call was to Quincy Jones, not to ask him if he wanted to produce the album but instead ask him if he could *suggest* the names of some producers who might be ideal! Quincy put forward just one name – his own. After pondering the suggestion for a short while, Michael called Quincy to agree – what would become the hottest pairing in music history had just got together on a more permanent basis.

While Michael had not seriously considered Quincy as the producer when he first thought about the album, the eventual pairing made sense. Michael had enjoyed working with Quincy on the soundtrack to *The Wiz*, finding his technique in the studio conducive to bringing the best out of Michael as a singer. Quincy also had the knack of being in the right place at the right time – he had learned his craft as a member of Lionel Hampton's band as a youngster, become the first black executive at a white record company when accepting a Vice Presidents role with Mercury Records, and had a vast experience of different musical styles having played jazz, scored films and produced other R&B acts. The five Grammy awards Quincy had won up to this point covered Best Instrumental Arrangement, Best Instrumental Jazz Performance, Best Contemporary Instrumental Performance and two awards for Best Instrumental Arrangement. Over the previous four or five years Quincy had also launched the hugely

successful career of the Johnson siblings, Louis and
George, and had guided them to a Grammy Award for
Best R&B Instrumental Performance for their track 'Q'
in 1977. The more Michael thought about it, the more he
realised Quincy was exactly the right man to helm his
all-important solo album.

While Michael had plenty of songs of his own up for
consideration for the album, Quincy had contacts that
at that time Michael could only dream of tapping into.
David Foster and Carole Bayer Sager sent over 'It's The
Falling In Love', Paul McCartney, no less, sent a tape of
'Girlfriend', Stevie Wonder submitted 'I Can't Help It',
and a song Quincy endorsed called 'She's Out Of My
Life' by singer-songwriter Tom Bahler all made the final
cut. The rest of the material came from two sources –
Michael and Rod Temperton. 'Don't Stop 'Til You Get
Enough' was a logical continuation of 'Shake Your Body'
and would become the obvious lead track for the album.
'Workin' Day And Night' and 'Get On The Floor'
(co-written by Michael and Louis Johnson) were
further nods towards the dance and disco set.

If the likes of Paul McCartney and Stevie Wonder were
household names, and other contributors at least well-
known within the music industry, the same could not be
said for Rod Temperton. The former keyboard player with
the mainly British soul group Heatwave, Rod had quickly
become the main songwriter, penning such uptempo hits
as 'Boogie Nights' and 'Too Hot To Handle' and the
sublime ballad 'Always And Forever'. Never entirely
comfortable on stage, Rod would eventually retire from
live work in order to concentrate on writing. It was at this
point he was asked to submit three songs for consideration
for the upcoming Michael Jackson solo album.

In an interview with this writer shortly after the release of *Thriller*, Rod stated that as well as performing live there were other aspects of his work he didn't particularly like – although he could write a mean melody, he positively hated writing lyrics! So much so that he claimed to enjoy working with Herbie Hancock more than any other artist, because Herbie didn't really require lyrics in his music! Yet Rod was professional enough to do his homework before writing material with Michael in mind, studying all of Michael's earlier albums to see what kind of phrasing would best suit his singing style and writing accordingly. The original intention was for Rod to submit three songs and for Michael and Quincy to select the best one for inclusion; in the end they loved all three and included them all.

These ten tracks were the ones that finally made it onto the album, after scores had been considered. The recording sessions went on and on, as both Quincy and Michael searched for perfection in every track. 'She's Out Of My Life', for example, was recorded and re-recorded on countless occasions, but each time Michael got around to the final lyrics, he would burst into tears. Eventually, Quincy reasoned that that was the impact the lyrics of the song were supposed to cause and left the tears on the recording. The other nine tracks were equally painstakingly crafted. 'I Can't Help It' might have been a relatively easy song for Stevie Wonder to sing, but the constant key changes were not something Michael was used to. Eventually, after taking what Quincy would describe as a lot of risks in both production techniques and song selection, Michael submitted the tapes to Epic for an August 1979 release.

Equal consideration was given to the artwork for the

cover. Ron Weisner and Freddy DeMann (two managers who had been appointed by Joseph to help him break The Jacksons into the big time) wanted to project a sophisticated image in keeping with the music on the album. 'The tuxedo was the overall plan for the *Off The Wall* project and package. The tuxedo was our idea, the socks were Michael.'

'Don't Stop 'Til You Get Enough' was not only the lead track on the album, it was released as the first single, hitting the shops in July that year. It proved an immediate success around the world, hitting the top of the charts in the US in October for a week and making #3 in the UK, where it would earn Michael his first solo silver award for sales in excess of 250,000 copies. When the album was finally released in August, it too shot up the charts, hitting #3 in the US and #5 in the UK. Epic on both sides of the Atlantic looked at the album as being laden with hits and potential hits, all of which would continue to service the album. In the UK, the title track 'Off The Wall' was chosen as the follow-up single, a decision vindicated when it too made the Top Ten, peaking at #7. In the US, Epic went with 'Rock With You' and hit the top again, dethroning KC & The Sunshine Band's 'Please Don't Go'.

Still the hits kept coming. 'Rock With You' made it a third consecutive Top Ten hit for Michael in the UK as it hit #7 while 'Off The Wall' made #10 in the US. And while many artists would have been content with pulling three top ten singles off one album, Michael went one better, becoming the first artist in history to have lifted as many as four Top Ten hits from the same album, when the stunningly emotional 'She's Out Of My Life' hit #3 in the UK and #10 in the US. A fifth single, 'Girlfriend' was issued in the UK but stalled at #41, a case of one too many for this particular album.

The extraordinary success of the singles only helped
sales of the album rather than deflate them. In the final
reckoning, *Off The Wall* shifted more than seven million
copies in the US and some 1.8 million in the UK on its
way to more than 20 million sales around the world.
Off The Wall wasn't only a commercial success either,
for the critical praise the album attracted was universal,
with one claiming that Michael Jackson was 'probably
the best singer in the world right now in terms of
style and technique.'

Come 1980 and the traditional awards ceremonies,
Michael expected to sweep up virtually all and sundry.
He bagged three American Music Awards and two at the
Billboard Music Awards and confidently expected to do
equally as well at the Grammy Awards. When he won
just the one, in the Best Male R&B Vocal Performance
category for 'Don't Stop 'Til You Get Enough', Michael
couldn't contain his disappointment. 'It was totally unfair
that it didn't get Record of the Year and it can never
happen again.'

Michael would have to wait for his next assault on the
Grammy Awards, for while *Off The Wall* was racking up
sales, Michael was back in the studio with his brothers
working on the next Jacksons album *Triumph*. The
importance of Michael to the continuing success and
earning capacity of his brothers was evident in the final
track listing of the album. Of the nine tracks on display,
Michael wrote or co-wrote six of them, including all four
that would eventually be released as singles.

Michael's presence undoubtedly helped sales of the
album, which would attain platinum status in the US
for sales of more than a million copies, their second
consecutive million-seller. In the UK it went gold

(sales of 100,000 plus), with two singles making the
Top Ten in 'Can You Feel It' and 'Walk Right Now' and
'Lovely One' making #29 and 'Heartbreak Hotel' #44.
The singles fared less well in the US, peaking at #77,
#73, #12 and #22 respectively. But singles success was
only a means to an end as far as Joseph was concerned;
there was more money to be made touring and he was
already formulating plans to get the boys on the road on
the *Triumph* tour. He wasn't to know it, but Michael was
making his own plans: he was shopping for a new lawyer,
one who could possibly act as a manager too!

Ever since the Jackson 5 had launched their career with
Motown, the boys had been happy to leave the business
side of things to Joseph and whoever he appointed to look
after their interests. This had caused some problems along
the way. Not one of the Jackson family had bothered to
read the original contract put in front of them by Motown
in 1969, with the result they had overlooked such matters
as being ultimately responsible for all the costs associated
with anything they recorded for the label. They'd also
missed the clause that stated that Motown owned the
rights to their name and could decide whether to replace
any member of the group if they saw fit. Given the age
of the boys when they signed, their oversight can be
forgiven, but for Joseph (and Katherine, his wife, who
also had to sign as a legal guardian) to have missed such
crucial elements of the contract could not. It had proven to
be an expensive mistake on his part. There had never been
any evidence that Joseph was skimming off the monies
coming in, but some of the deals that the boys found
themselves saddled with were not the kind of deals they
would have chosen if it had been left up to them. While
they lived at home they danced to Joseph's tune, but as

they left to get married or, as in Michael's case, generated their own income, they demanded more independence. Michael began putting his shopping list together by speaking to his accountant to get the names of three entertainment lawyers worthy of talking to. The intention was to speak to all three and chose the best one; in the end Michael signed up with the only one he spoke to, John Branca.

Joseph was devastated when he learned Michael had appointed his own lawyer, perhaps realising this was just the first step in losing his son as a client. In truth, that process had begun the first time he raised his fist to Michael when he was a little boy. Michael had grown to positively hate his father, not only for the way he treated him and his siblings while they were trying to do their best to learn their routines, but more importantly for the way he had treated Katherine over the years. Joseph's attraction to other women had not diminished over the years. There was a steady stream of young females eager to get close to any of the Jacksons. If Jackie, or Marlon, or Michael or Tito or any of the brothers weren't attainable, then the father would do... Joseph had been the same when the boys were starting out in Gary, bringing women back to the small hotel rooms the boys were sharing and expecting them to keep quiet to their mother about what was happening out on the road. As the boys became more successful, so the women who tried to attach themselves to the group became more attractive. Joseph was known to have had at least one relationship that had resulted in a miscarriage and would later have another than would result in the birth of a daughter. All of this was ammunition that Michael stored up before he finally cut the ties that bound him to Joseph.

Touring with his brothers was the last thing on Michael's mind in 1980. The success of his *Off The Wall* album had convinced him that his future lay with a solo career; doing the *Triumph* tour was a distraction he could live without. Michael was changing, both as an artist and as a person, having recently had a second operation on his nose. Always sensitive about his looks and having suffered terribly from acne as a boy, Michael had had his first nose operation after breaking it following a fall while working on a dance routine. He then suffered some breathing problems and opted to have a second operation. This he deemed was a success, in part because it made him look less like his father than he had before the operation!

Michael eventually felt compelled to join his brothers for the *Triumph* tour; Joseph couldn't have cared less whether Michael's heart wasn't into it, only that his body was! It proved to be little more than a distraction to Michael, who was eager to get back into the studio as projects began to rack up for him to consider. There was a storybook version of *ET*, already his favourite film, that he wanted to do as a favour to Steven Spielberg (it would eventually earn Michael a Grammy Award for Best Recording for Children). There was also the opportunity to write and produce for his favourite artist, Diana Ross. Her career since leaving Motown for RCA Records had stalled and she had called Michael to suggest they might work together. Michael penned and produced 'Muscles', a song inspired by his pet boa constrictor!

The *Triumph* tour was eventually captured on tape and duly released as the double album *The Jacksons Live* at the end of the year. Recorded during dates in Memphis, New York City and Atlanta, the album would hit #30 in the US, and a rather more modest #53 in the UK. The tour was a commercial success, boosting the rest of the Jacksons' financial fortunes, but would prove to be the last tour the brothers did together in four years.

In August 1982, Michael and Quincy got together again to begin work on the follow-up album to *Off The Wall*. The success of the earlier album had raised expectations and the bar. The new album was given a production budget of $750,000 – at that time a colossal amount of money. First off, Michael and Quincy sifted their way through some 300 or so songs that were up for consideration, before finally whittling down the number to a rather more manageable nine to record!

Michael was to write four of the tracks on the finished album, including 'Wanna Be Startin' Somethin'', 'Beat It' and 'Billie Jean'. After the relative success of 'Girlfriend' from the earlier album, Paul McCartney had called Michael and suggest they record something together. Michael had penned the mid-tempo 'The Girl Is Mine' specifically with Paul and himself in mind. 'Billie Jean' came to Michael as a result of a obsessive fan – he began getting letters at home from a girl who claimed to be madly in love with Michael, so much so that she had just given birth to their child! Michael hadn't even met the girl, little less been intimate with her, but it did not stop her writing almost non-stop and sending him pictures of herself at graduation and other pictures of their alleged child. When he received a package that contained a gun and the message that Michael should shoot himself on a specific date at a specific time, as she intended doing, it was time to call in the authorities. Still, it made great material for a song.

'Beat It' was a deliberate attempt to write something that would cross over from Michael's traditional R&B fanbase into the white rock market, while 'Wanna Be Startin' Somethin'' sounded much like his earlier work simply because it was written around the same period as 'Get On The Floor' and 'Working Night And Day'.

As they had done with *Off The Wall*, Quincy and Michael had cast their net far and wide looking for the right kind of material. Steve Porcaro, a member of Toto who would provide much of the musical accompaniment to the album, linked with John Bettis to pen 'Human Nature' and Quincy wrote 'PYT (Pretty Young Thing)' with another of his protégés, James Ingram. The final three tracks came from Rod Temperton. Whether Temperton was asked to submit three for consideration, before they would be scaled down to one, has not been revealed!

Despite the success Quincy and Michael had enjoyed with the first album, relationships between the two were rather strained this time around. To begin with, Michael was becoming his own man in the studio now. He had his own ideas as to how the songs should sound, especially so on the titles he had composed himself. 'Billie Jean' was a case in point: Quincy suggested shortening the introduction to make it a short and perhaps tighter number, but Michael was insistent – the lengthy introduction made him feel like dancing and he felt it would have the same impact with his audience. Well then, said Quincy, what about the title – it would make people think of the tennis star Billie Jean King, so why not change it to 'Not My Lover'? Michael asked his sister LaToya what she thought of the suggestion – did she think of tennis when she heard the title 'Billie Jean'? LaToya confirmed she didn't, so Michael insisted the title remain as he had written it.

Both agreed that 'Beat It' needed a top rock guitarist to really make the number, but couldn't think or find anyone who fitted the role perfectly until Eddie Van Halen came on board. 'I wrote a song called 'Beat It' and we wanted a great solo, a guitar solo, so that night Quincy said I have a great idea, someone like Van Halen would be a good idea or Pete Townshend, but Townshend and The Who were touring at that moment so we thought it would be a problem. So the next day, the very next day Eddie was in the studio. He's the kind of guy that kept worrying that his part was okay and he wanted to be just right. He's a perfectionist.' Eddie Van Halen was indeed perfection on what would be described as Michael's homage to *West Side Story*.

The Rod Temperton song that would eventually become the title of the album was a fairly typical Temperton song with an extremely strong hook but with effects added that turned the number into a mini operatic piece. Originally working on the title 'Starlight' or 'Midnight Man', Rod settled on calling the song 'Thriller' because he thought it had merchandising potential! While 'Thriller' was strong enough to have got away without it, someone suggested getting a well known horror actor to do a monologue at the end of the track to further add to the image of a thriller. Rod wrote the monologue that would eventually be recorded by Vincent Price while sitting in the taxi on his way to the studio! As Michael said at the time 'I've known Vincent ever since I was 11 years old. And when you think of 'Thriller'...I mean who's the king of horror who's still alive? I mean Bela Lugosi and Peter Lorre are dead now and the only giant who goes back to those days is Vincent Price, so I thought he was the perfect voice... it was Rod and Quincy who actually thought of him because he's a friend and everything. He came in right away, it was no problem.'

The other tracks Rod contributed were ballads reminiscent of 'Always And Forever'; 'Baby Be Mine' and 'The Lady In My Life', the album's stunning closer.

When Quincy and Michael sat down to listen to the finished album, Michael was moved to tears – it was awful, just awful. The sound wasn't right, and all the work they had put in to recording it had been wasted. Each and every track would have to be completely remixed before Michael was satisfied. When Walter Yetnikoff was informed that there was going to be a delay he was far from happy. This was an important album for CBS, and whatever else happened it *had* to be on the market before the end of the year in order to sweep up Christmas sales. Any further delay would not be tolerated – the album had to appear in December, come what may.

While Quincy and Michael set about remixing the album, the tapes for the opening single were sent to Epic to ready for release. 'The Girl Is Mine' played much on the fact that it was a collaboration between Michael and Paul McCartney – it was a mid-tempo song about a supposed feud between Michael and Paul who desired the same girl. Released as a single in November 1982, it would make #2 in the US and #8 in the UK, respectable enough positions given the presence of two worldwide superstars, but hardly a ringing endorsement for the album that was to follow.

CHAPTER SIX

THRILLER

At the time *Thriller* was released around the world, I was working as a Press Officer for the CBS label in London. It was usual whenever a major album was about to drop, be it on CBS or Epic, for the marketing staff of whichever label to host a listening party for their colleagues on the other label. Thus CBS had played host to their Epic counterparts for Adam & The Ants *Prince Charming* and Epic would reciprocate on Michael's *Thriller*.

There were no pictures of the artwork, so the elegant and suave image that had been started with *Off The Wall* and would continue with *Thriller* would not be revealed until finished copies were pressed. Similarly, there were no videos to watch – the album would have to stand or fall, at least as far as the critical view of CBS employees were concerned, with the music. The album kicked off with 'Wanna Be Startin' Somethin'' and nearly 40 minutes later finished with 'The Lady In My Life'. And as far as more than a few present were concerned, there wasn't too much to get excited about. Even senior executives within CBS expressed their disappointment with the album – there didn't appear to be anything as instantly catchy as 'Rock With You' or 'Off The Wall', no stunning dance track like 'Don't Stop 'Til You Get Enough' and no tearjerker to match 'She's Out Of My Life'. In short, *Thriller* hardly appeared to live up to its title.

Apparently, much the same reaction had occurred in the studio when Michael and Quincy played the album for Ron Weisner and Freddy DeMann. Both managers tried to tell Michael that the music industry had changed, that sales were down all across the board and *Thriller* might have to settle for selling about two million copies if he was lucky. It was not what Michael wanted to hear (and effectively spelt the end of Ron and Freddy as co-managers of Michael with their father Joseph). Quincy Jones also incurred the wrath of Michael for daring to agree with the assessment of the album's chances in the market, although he would at least remain within the camp for a few more years.

Furious with the reaction he had got from those supposedly closest to him, Michael threatened to pull the album, instructing John Branca to get Walter Yetnikoff to call him and see what he thought of potential sales. At the time, Walter would need two million sales minimum to help get CBS through a difficult time in the American music market, so two million copies would be better than none at all if Michael pulled the album! So Walter called and placated his artist: CBS would do all and everything in its power to ensure the record was as big a success as it possibly could. Relieved, Michael gave the go ahead for the album to be released.

After the limited success of 'The Girl Is Mine', Michael had decided that 'Billie Jean' would be the follow-up single. Still a relatively new medium, videos had become an important tool in getting the artist and his music over to markets that he couldn't physically attend to, so Michael drafted in Steve Barron and Simon Fields as director and producer respectively for the song. Michael had no idea what he wanted to feature in the video, so Steve Barron came up with a simple storyline of Michael being stalked by a photographer, added a stretch of pavement that lit up as Michael walked across it and got Michael to do what he was best at, dance. The end result was as simple as it could be; there was nothing contentious, nothing outrageous, nothing that could cause offence to anyone.

Yet CBS struggled to get the video on MTV, the music-video-only channel that had gone on air in 1981 and positioned itself as something of a rock channel. Few if any black artists had their videos shown on the channel, and more than a few artists were disturbed at what they saw as a colour bar. On the one hand, there was no evidence that customers who were subscribing to MTV were only white teenagers, but the fact that the music they were being shown was only by white artists caused consternation across the industry. Epic's promotional executives submitted the 'Billie Jean' video more in hope than in expectation and got knocked back on the grounds that it wasn't what the core MTV audience was buying. When word got back to Walter Yetnikoff, he decided to take matters into his own hands. Calling up the head of MTV, he demanded to know why Michael's video wasn't going to be shown and got the stock core audience excuse. That wasn't good enough for Walter. 'I'm not going to give you any more videos and I'm going to go public and tell them about the fact you don't want to play music by a black guy.'

If Berry Gordy had been the one making the call, MTV could have afforded to call his bluff, since the only music Berry could offer was black music! But Walter had several aces up his sleeve – if MTV wouldn't play Michael Jackson then they wouldn't be getting Bruce Springsteen, Toto, Men At Work, or any other video from the company. And Walter would tell the world why he'd pulled all of his artists off the channel. In the end MTV had little or no option to back down, especially if they wanted access to the rock giants in the future. MTV could have put the video on a couple of times or on mid rotation, but perhaps sensing that Yetnikoff was mad enough at them to carry through his threat to go public, they added the video on heavy rotation. Having already proven to be well on its way to becoming a major hit without MTV's aid, it would top the US charts for seven weeks. It would also top the UK charts for a week during that American run, giving Michael a satisfying double success.

While Walter Yetnikoff was on the phone to his counterpart at MTV, Michael was having to field calls from assorted family and friends regarding an upcoming television special dedicated to Motown. Suzanne De Passe's idea, timed to coincide with Motown's 25th anniversary, the hope had been that the bigger names who had left Motown over the years would reunite for one evening's celebration. The plan had been a good one, but getting some of the artists to put aside their differences with Berry Gordy, even for one evening, was proving a difficult task. In many cases, while Suzanne De Passe had been (and continued to be) a highly respected executive within Motown, the artists concerned felt that if Berry Gordy wanted them to be there then he should be the one extending the invitations. So Berry was pressed into action to try to get the hold outs to agree to turn up – without Marvin Gaye, Diana Ross and the Jackson 5 in general and Michael Jackson in particular it wouldn't be much of a show.

Marvin and Diana proved relatively easy to get across the line. Michael proved more stubborn. Michael had nothing personal against Berry Gordy. When the Jackson 5 were engineering their exit from Motown, he had gone behind his father's back and met with Berry to discuss the situation, an astonishing thing for an 18-year-old young man to do, but proof that Michael respected Berry for all he had done for the group in their early days. But Michael felt he was being used. The brothers needed him to appear and Joseph needed him to appear, and he didn't feel much like helping either party out.

Berry did what Michael had done eight years earlier – he paid him a visit. Michael was in the Motown studio working on a remix when Berry popped in to talk. After a while chatting over old times and memories, Berry came to the point – he needed Michael to appear with his brothers and sing the Motown hits. Michael thought for a moment and said he would do it, but on the proviso that he could then sing solo. Berry was excited at the prospect and agreed instantly, but Michael sensed Berry had misconstrued what he meant – he wasn't go to sing 'Got To Be There' or 'Rockin' Robin' or any of his Motown hits; he wanted to sing his new songs like 'Billie Jean'. Berry told him it didn't fit into the concept of the evening - Marvin Gaye was going to be there but he would be singing material like 'What's Going On', not his new stuff like 'Sexual Healing'. Michael was insistent; it was his way with 'Billie Jean' or no way. Reluctantly, Berry was forced to concede, reasoning that Michael Jackson singing what he wanted had to be better than no Michael Jackson singing at all. With hindsight, it turned out to be one of the greatest decisions Berry Gordy ever made where Michael Jackson was concerned, even if he didn't realise it at the time.

Michael could have gone on the show, which was taped at the Civic Center in Los Angeles on 25 April 1983, sung with his brothers on a medley of their Motown hits and then sung 'Billie Jean' and received the expected applause from the audience. It would have helped Motown and it

would have helped sales of *Thriller* into the bargain. But
Michael had bigger things in store. Always fascinated by
new dance moves, Michael remembered watching *Soul
Train* when he was younger and in particular a move
that had been performed some three years earlier, then
'retired'. It was then known as backsliding and Michael
tracked down the dancer who had performed it on the
show, Casper, and asked him to teach him the move.
Casper agreed, for which he got a fee of $1,000. He taught
the rudiments of the move to Michael over a couple of
days, even though Michael could never quite seem to get it
right in the rehearsal studio. Casper went along to see The
Jacksons live when they hit town and Michael still didn't
introduce the move into the set, telling Casper afterwards
that he still hadn't nailed it.

Casper was one of millions who settled down to watch
the nostalgia special *Motown 25 – Yesterday, Today and
Forever*. Just as he had promised Berry Gordy, Michael
joined with his brothers (including Jermaine, the first time
the original line-up had reunited since their acrimonious
parting eight years previously) for a medley of their
Motown hits. As the music came to an end, the other
Jackson brothers headed for the wings as Michael took
centre stage. 'Those were magic moments with all my
brothers – including Jermaine. But, you know, those were
the good songs. I like those songs a lot. But especially I
like… the new songs.'

The crowd knew what was coming, 'Billie Jean'. Or
the crowd *thought* they knew what was coming, for the
next three minutes or so would become one of the greatest
performances ever witnessed. As the intro started, it
became obvious that Michael was going to lip synch his
performance, so whatever he had in mind was going to

have to be special. Constantly on the move with a variety of dance moves, Michael was still giving little or nothing away – most of the moves he was doing were the kind of moves that he had done for years as part of the Jackson 5/Jacksons. Then, as the song reached its instrumental bridge came the moment that transformed Michael's career forever; a spin, a little hitch of his trousers (which were short anyway so the audience could see his gleaming socks in between his black trousers and shoes) and an effortless glide backwards across the stage. Those in the audience who weren't already on their feet leapt up and screamed while in the wings the rest of the family stood open-mouthed at what they had just witnessed. Just in case there was anyone who had missed it the first time around, Michael repeated the move towards the end of the song, further setting him apart from the rest of the competition. It is debatable as to who benefited more from their respective moonwalks, Neil Armstrong or Michael Jackson, but that evening at the Civic Centre witnessed the birth of a legend. Michael's life and pop music would never be the same after that stunning glide across stage.

Thriller may have been released at a time when the entire industry, not just CBS, was in the doldrums, but after that performance sales began to crank up. And up. And up again. And there was still more to come. When in 1980 Michael had asked *Rolling Stone* magazine if they were interested in interviewing him and putting him on the cover, they had turned him down. 'I've been told over and over that black people on the cover doesn't sell copies. Just wait. Someday those magazines are going to be begging me for an interview. Maybe I'll give them one. And maybe I won't.' After the Motown performance, *every* magazine wanted Michael for the cover. Some he gave interviews to and, just as promised, some he didn't.

The success of *Thriller* didn't just impact on CBS either. The then President of A&M Records Gil Friesen stated 'The whole industry has a stake in this success.' When customers went into their local record stores to buy *Thriller*, they often bought more than just the Michael Jackson album they'd gone in for. If any one man can be said to have turned the fortunes of an industry around, then that man was Michael Jackson. At its peak, *Thriller* was selling over a *million* copies a week around the world! Little wonder that it was to spend a total of 37 weeks at the top of the US charts. By comparison, *Saturday Night Fever,* the best selling album in the world up to that point, topped the charts for only 24 weeks. *Sgt Pepper* by the Beatles had managed only 15 weeks and *A Hard Day's Night* a mere 14. And even the best selling Elvis album, *Blue Hawaii* had only topped the chart for twenty weeks. *Thriller* was a phenomenon from another planet altogether.

Michael may not have had much of an idea over what to do with the video for 'Billie Jean', but he sure knew what he wanted for 'Beat It'. Written as a counter to gang violence, he asked his assistants to enlist the help of a number of members of rival Los Angeles gangs and put together a story around the theme that violence can be beaten by dancing. Only Michael Jackson could have got away with it, but as he said at the time 'The point is no one has to be the tough guy, you can walk away from a fight and still be a man.' The dance routines, worked out by Michael and Michael Peters, turned the video into an event and helped send the single sailing to the top of the charts. Indeed, had the video appeared a week earlier, the chances are Michael would have replaced *himself* at number one on the singles chart, for 'Billie Jean' had been dethroned a week earlier by Dexys Midnight Runners and 'Come On Eileen'. In the UK, 'Beat It' had to be content with a #3 placing.

Every time *Thriller* looked like it might be running out of steam, along would come another single to propel it back up the charts or continue its strangle hold on the top spot. More importantly, every one of the seven tracks eventually lifted from the album hit the Top Ten of the Billboard charts, an event without precedent. After 'Beat It' came 'Wanna Be Startin' Somethin'' (#5), 'Human Nature' (#7), 'PYT' (#10) and finally 'Thriller' (#4). In between 'PYT' and 'Thriller' Michael topped the charts with the second half of his duet with Paul McCartney; reciprocating Paul's help on 'The Girl Is Mine' Michael joined with Paul on his single 'Say Say Say' and spent six weeks at the summit. In the UK, 'Wanna Be Startin'' Somethin'' peaked at #8, 'Thriller' at #10, PYT at #11 and 'Say Say Say' in between them hit #2. 'Human Nature' was not released as a single in the UK but still became something of a turntable hit on radio.

If *West Side Story* had been the inspiration for 'Beat It', then *An American Werewolf In London* proved to be the inspiration for 'Thriller', at least as far as the video was concerned. Michael called John Landis, the film's director, to ask him if he would direct the video for his seventh and final single release from the album of the same name. John Landis agreed, and the pair quickly realised that the grandiose plans they had put in place for the video were way beyond the budgets of a mere pop single. By their reckoning, the video was likely to come in at $600,000 – a standard pop video would normally cost a fifth of that. There was no way the record company could justify that

kind of spend and no way Michael could afford that kind
of outlay – money was rolling in thanks to *Thriller* but it
seemed the height of folly to spend so much on one video.
So Michael and John Branca thought about how they
could raise the money from elsewhere. The pair came up
with the idea of extending the shooting so that there would
be enough material in order to create a secondary film, *The
Making Of Thriller*. They sold the idea to Vestron Video
and got them to stump $500,000 for the exclusive video
distribution rights to the video when it was made. With
the Vestron deal in place, Branca then contacted MTV and
told them about this documentary Michael was making
and that if they wanted to air it then they would have to
pay. Having previously been given videos by artists for
nothing because they wanted them played, it must have
surprised MTV to be asked to pay for the privilege with
'Thriller', but when it was explained that they would
be getting a world exclusive for an agreed period, MTV
agreed to contribute another $500,000. Which was just as
well as the final cost of 'Thriller' was to hit in excess
of $1 million.

Just as Michael's performance on the Motown special
became an event, so did the release of the *Thriller* video.
Unlike anything ever seen previously, *Thriller* set the
benchmark for not only Michael but for just about every
other pop music video that came after. Yet the whole
project nearly got shelved. Filming had finished and
editing and mixing were being undertaken to turn the
video into a virtual film release when elders at the Encino
Kingdom Hall, a Jehovah's Witness church where Michael
and his mother attended, heard about the video and
requested a meeting with Michael. The subject matter of
the video, if what they had heard was correct, concerned

them and Michael should either change it or issue a statement setting out his beliefs. Michael refused. So the church threatened to banish him altogether. And Michael got scared.

When he eventually spoke to John Branca (Michael apparently made at least four or five calls but wouldn't or couldn't speak when the telephone was answered), he asked him to destroy the tapes. When Branca enquired why, Michael told him about the threat to banish him from the church, since the content of the video was at odds with their religious beliefs. He wouldn't listen to any argument from John as to how the video was not an endorsement for the afterlife or ghouls, merely a pop video and instructed him again to destroy the tapes as soon as possible. John didn't destroy them, although he would later tell Michael he had in order to put his mind at ease, at least temporarily.

Then John Branca happened to read an article about Bela Lugosi, an actor who made virtually an entire career out of playing Dracula and similar characters in a succession of horror films. Yet Bela Lugosi was equally religious and obviously had no trouble separating his religious beliefs from his acting self. John rang Michael and engaged him in a conversation about Bela Lugosi and told him the story of his religion and acting. John then said that if Michael or the church had a problem with how the video might be construed, why not put a disclaimer on the front to the effect that the video was not reflective of Michael or his beliefs. Michael thought it a masterstroke and even forgave John Branca for obviously lying to him over destroying the tapes. So the video that aired opened with the legend 'Due to my strong personal convictions, I wish to stress that this film in no way endorses a belief in the occult.'

The video duly received its exclusive airing on MTV and sales of the subsequently released *The Making Of Thriller* went through the same roof the *Thriller* album had already disappeared through. Just before the release of the video, the album was shifting some 200,000 copies a week, a still healthy figure for an album that was already a year old. After the screening of the 14-minute video on MTV, sales shot back up to 600,000 a week. *Thriller* would go on to set many records, including being one of only three albums to have been the bestselling album in America in two separate years (1983 and 1984) and one of only three albums to have remained in the Top Ten for a whole year – *Thriller* would stretch that particular record to 80 consecutive weeks in the Top Ten.

Accurate sales figures for *Thriller* have proved almost impossible to ascertain. How much is record company manipulation and how much is sheer exaggeration is equally mired in confusion. The facts that are known are these: in the US, the album is certified as having sold over 28 million copies (although it has been overtaken as the best selling album in the US, with The Eagles' *Greatest Hits* having shifted an extra million copies). In the UK, where it topped the charts for a mere eight weeks, the album is certified 11 times platinum for sales in excess of 3.3 million copies. Add to these figures sales in just about every other country in the world and the total falls *somewhere* between the claimed 47 and 109 million copies! Perhaps the closest estimate comes from the 'Guinness Book of World Records', which holds *Thriller* to be the best selling album with sales of 65 million copies as of 2007. And those were the sales figures before Michael's death; sales of his entire catalogue picked up following news of his untimely demise.

CHAPTER SEVEN

...AND THE WINNER IS...

*T*hriller* may have been a commercial and critical success, but what Michael craved more than anything else at that time was recognition from his peers. After the debacle of *Off The Wall* four years earlier, Michael hoped he would not have a wasted journey when he attended the Grammy Awards in 1984. It was certainly looking good; seven trophies at the American Music Awards held at the Shrine Auditorium in January was an unprecedented feat and put Michael in good heart for the forthcoming Grammys.

Michael very nearly didn't make it to the ceremony. In October 1983, Michael had caved in to pressure from his family and agreed to participate in a 1984 tour to be called 'The Victory Tour' – after the name of the forthcoming Jacksons album. Michael didn't want to do the tour for a number of reasons, not least because he now saw himself as a solo artist who had previously been a member of a family group, not the other way around. For his brothers, however, touring with Michael would give them all an opportunity to line their pockets quite considerably. Who wasn't going to want to come out and watch the man who had virtually changed recording history? Without a manager in place, there was no one between Michael and his family to fend off questions about whether he would commit. He told each of his brothers who called that he had no intention of touring, he told Joseph the same when he called, but when his mother Katherine called, his attitude softened. Joseph had decided that the family would be promoting this tour, thus keeping more of the revenue for themselves, and had named his wife as one of the co-promoters; when she told Michael that she needed him to tour, he reluctantly agreed.

Hindsight shows that Michael should have stuck to his original decision. This wasn't even intended to be a tour with good intentions, but simply a money making exercise for the Jackson family. What started as a bad idea got steadily worse with each passing day. Perhaps realising that he wasn't fully up to the job of organising such as massive tour (and with Michael in tow it would be massive), Joseph had looked for outside assistance. Although there were plenty of competent tour organisers, people who did this kind of thing for a living, Joseph decided to align himself with Don King. Perhaps best known as the former manager and promoter of boxer Muhammad Ali, Don King evoked different reactions from different people. To some he was the consummate showman. His press conferences invariably attracted considerable media coverage, simply because he could usually be relied upon to say something that was media worthy. Yet there were nagging doubts about his ethics as a businessman, with many of his former clients having to forcibly extract themselves from his clutches at some point during their careers.

King had organised a press conference in November at the Tavern On The Green in New York to announce the 18-city, 40-date tour by all six Jackson brothers (Jermaine was rejoining the group after the success of the reunion earlier in the year). What came next left Michael horrified. Tickets for the events could only be bought in blocks of four, with each ticket costing $30 each (the average cost of a ticket to see Bruce Springsteen, who would also be on tour at much the same time, was $16). Potential buyers would have to buy the $120 money orders and send them off to an address and wait and see if the application had been successful. If it was, the tickets would duly be sent, if not, the money eventually returned. It was this aspect that caused the most consternation. Someone would be sitting on a large pile of money and earning interest on it before it had to be returned to the unsuccessful customer. That was not the way Michael believed in going about business. Then there was the announcement that Pepsi Cola were sponsoring the tour to the tune of $5 million. In return, Michael and his brothers would be expected to produce two commercials for the company. No one had cleared this with Michael before the announcement was made, and he wasn't particularly happy about it – he didn't even drink the stuff!

Michael was eventually able to get the ticketing arrangements amended, almost to his satisfaction. Once it was accepted that many of his fans would be unable to afford the $120, it was agreed to sell the tickets singularly. Michael also ensured that a percentage of the tickets were handed out for free to under-privileged fans in each city. He was unable to get out of the Pepsi deal. Perhaps working on the assumption that if you can't beat them then join them, Michael agreed to do the commercials but only if he got to produce them. Pepsi would get the use of 'Billie Jean' with specially-written lyrics, but Michael could control how much or how little his face appeared on screen. Pepsi excitedly agreed and gave the go-ahead.

Filming for the first commercial was scheduled for 26-27 January at the Shrine Auditorium, where 4000 lucky fans had been given free tickets to come along and participate as an audience for the two days. During the

second day's filming and on the sixth take of a particular
scene, a spark ignited his hair and Michael, initially
unaware that his hair was on fire, continued his routine.
Miko Brando (Marlon's son), working as a bodyguard
for Michael was the first to react, rushing on stage and
dousing the flames. An ambulance took Michael to the
Cedars-Sinai Medical Center, where it was revealed he
had suffered second degree burns to his skull. Michael
would eventually make a full recovery from the incident
and receive $1.5 million in compensation from Pepsi,
which he subsequently donated to the Brotman Memorial
Hospital, where the Michael Jackson Burns Center was
established. Footage of the incident was suppressed at
the time, perhaps to ensure no adverse publicity towards
PepsiCo, but was subsequently released following
Michael's death some 25 years later. The footage revealed
that Michael had suffered a sizeable burn to the top of
his skull, and had been given pain killing drugs in the
immediate aftermath. He would come to rely on these
drugs for the rest of his life.

Michael recovered in time to attend the Grammy
Awards on 28 February, but he was still troubled.
According to Walter Yetnikoff, Michael telephoned
him shortly before the awards to see if he could use his
influence to ensure that certain awards went his way
– in particular Michael felt that Quincy Jones didn't
particularly deserve his nomination for Producer of the
Year since Michael had done most of the work on *Thriller*.
(Those who attended Michael's session with Diana Ross
on 'Muscles', where Michael *was* supposed to have been
producer, stated that he never gave Diana any direction
whatsoever, almost appearing in awe of the artist he was
supposed to be directing!). In Walter's account, he listened

incredulously as Michael reeled off a list of awards he felt he was most deserving of and then proceeded to tell him how the voting had already been conducted and Michael would have to sit and take his chance like everyone else!

Michael needn't have worried. Topping the list with 12 nominations in ten categories (Michael was up against himself in two of them!), he would make seven trips to the podium to collect the miniature statuette, including Album of the Year, Record of the Year and Best Rock Vocal Performance for 'Beat It', Best Pop Vocal Performance for 'Thriller', Best Rhythm & Blues Song and Best Rhythm & Blues Vocal Performance for 'Billie Jean', Best Recording for Children for *E.T. The Extra-Terrestrial* and Producer of the Year, sharing this latter award with Quincy Jones. If Michael was disappointed with Yetnikoff's lack of influence over the voting committee then he didn't show it, dragging Walter up on stage when he went to collect one award (Walter ensured the CBS hierarchy were aware of Michael's depth of feeling for the executive by extracting a hefty increase in his salary!). Even Bruce Swedien, the engineer on *Thriller*, received an award, thus confirming *Thriller* as the most successful album of all time.

While Pepsi had not been ultimately responsible for the accident that had occurred a month earlier, even if they had stumped up compensation, Michael felt he had been forced to do the commercial because of outside pressure. He was also disappointed to see that Motown had jumped on the bandwagon he had created by releasing old material and presenting it as though it was new – and there was nothing he could do to prevent it reaching the market. The best way to protect himself against such pressure in the future would be to have a manager. John Branca had undertaken many of the roles normally associated with the role since Michael had fired his father, but Branca was a lawyer and was kept busy dealing with Michael's growing business interests. So interviews were held to find a new manager for Michael. Candidates included Colonel Tom Parker, who had previously managed Elvis Presley. Despite talking to many others with vast experience, Michael would eventually opt for the most inexperienced – Frank Dileo, the then Head of Promotion at Epic Records. Michael felt much of the success for the album and singles from *Thriller* had been down to the aggressive way Frank had pushed them to radio and television. Michael first asked Frank if he was interested in managing him in August 1983 and repeated that offer in February the following year. This time around Frank agreed. Both Joseph and Don King would discover that Frank's lack of experience as a manager did not make him a soft touch when it came to getting Michael to do their bidding. Not by a long way....

The battle-lines were drawn early on. Frank told Michael of Don's reputation, especially how virtually all of Don's promotions seemed to earn *him* a lot of money but left everyone else out of pocket. Michael decided to issue a series of terms and conditions relating to how and what Don could do relevant to Michael. Don wasn't happy and made a number of statements claiming that Michael was being swayed by the opinions of a white lawyer (John Branca) and white manager (Dileo), which only added to Michael's fury.

As Michael had predicted, the 'Victory' tour was anything but a victory, at least as far as he was concerned. Sure, it made considerable sums of money for the rest of his family (Michael would donate virtually all of his fees and income to charity) and should have set them up for the rest of their lives with the income they banked, yet Michael sensed that at some point in the future, there would be further demands from his family to go out on the road 'one last time'. Where the family had once been close, this tour had only exposed the how much they had grown apart. They lived different lives to him and had different ways of going about their business, none of which Michael found tasteful. There was constant bickering throughout the tour, some of which Michael was responsible for, most of which he wasn't.

There were a couple of high points during the year, none of which were connected with Michael's brothers or their tour. Having received a telegram from President Reagan following his hospitalisation after the Pepsi incident, Michael received another when he was inducted into the Guinness Book of Records in February at the Museum of Natural History in New York. These two telegrams, from the US President no less, prompted a subsequent visit to the White House in May to meet with the President and his wife Nancy to receive the Presidential Humanitarian Award (the award was actually the idea of someone within Michael's camp, not the White House). Then came the news that Michael was to be awarded a star on the Hollywood Walk of Fame, with the induction taking place at 6927 Hollywood Boulevard in November.

The year also saw the release of the *Victory* album, supposedly the reason why the brothers were going out on the road. The prevalent atmosphere in the studio would be maintained throughout the tour. Although this was the first time all six brothers appeared on the same album, it was not a happy unit. Michael would write or co-write only three tracks on the album, including the lead single 'State Of Shock', which also featured Mick Jagger, which would make #3 in the US and #14 in the UK. The other two singles lifted, 'Torture' and 'Body' were written by Jackie with Kathy Wakefield and Marlon respectively, and while videos were made of both these latter singles, neither Michael nor Jermaine appeared in either. Yet despite all of the bickering and arguing and antagonism they all felt towards one another, *Victory* would eventually become the biggest selling album the boys ever had, hitting #4 in the US (and #3 in the UK). It sold more than two million copies, earning the group a double platinum award. Perhaps some of Michael's stardust had landed on the rest of the family too.

The 'Victory' tour finally came to an end on 9 December 1984 in Los Angeles. As it had headed towards the finale, Michael had sensed that his family and Don King hoped to be able to take the tour abroad, where there would undoubtedly be further riches to be made. Michael had done this tour as a favour to his mother and had no wish to spend any more of his time than was absolutely necessary out on the road. So when the final song finished, Michael made sure everyone knew where he stood as he announced on stage 'This is our last and final show. It's been a long 20 years and we love you all.' His brothers were surprised and Don King in a rage as Michael had just pulled the rug out from underneath them all – his plans were all about *his* career and future, not theirs.

As it happened, the very next task Michael undertook did involve many of his siblings. That summer reports had come in that a major famine had hit Ethiopia, with news reports from the area revealing that thousands, if not millions, were either dying or starving. Bob Geldof and Midge Ure had galvanised the British music industry with their single 'Do They Know It's Christmas', a single that had topped the UK charts and would make #13 in the US. The chart placings were unimportant; what mattered was the millions of pounds made to try to alleviate some of the famine. There were many within the American music industry, especially among the black artists, who felt that *they* should have responded quicker rather than allow the British to steal a march. Harry Belafonte for one was trying to get a number of artists together for a similarly-styled single, but was making little headway until he mentioned his plan to Ken Kragen, manager of Lionel Richie and Kenny Rogers, to see if he could get his clients interested. Lionel was immediately agreeable, also calling Stevie Wonder to get him aboard, and then Michael to see if he could be counted upon. Michael not only wanted to sing, he offered to help Lionel write the song.

Lionel made several trips up to Hayvenhurst to work on the song with Michael. Both wanted to produce something that had the feel of an anthem, something that would resonate around the world, and on 25 January, a night before the planned recording session, finished the song that would become 'We Are The World'. The following evening a host of artists at the American Music Awards came straight to the A&M Studios, including Lionel Richie, Stevie Wonder, Paul Simon, Kenny Rogers, James Ingram, Tina Turner, Billy Joel, Michael Jackson, Diana Ross, Dionne Warwick, Willie Nelson, Al Jarreau, Bruce Springsteen, Kenny Loggins, Steve Perry, Daryl Hall, Huey Lewis, Cyndi Lauper, Kim Carnes, Bob Dylan and Ray Charles. Also included on the night were Bob Geldof, the man behind the British version, and Michael's siblings Marlon, Jackie, Tito, Randy and LaToya. The recording took just two hours to complete, a remarkable feat given the sheer number of soloists on the record. There again, a sign outside the studio as the artists arrived stated 'Please check your egos at the door.'

Rush-released as a single almost immediately, 'We Are The World' by USA For Africa (which stood for United Support of Artists For Africa) topped the US charts for four weeks and the UK for two, selling more than four million copies domestically. The success of the single would be reflected in the following year's Grammy Awards, being named Record of the Year and Best Pop Vocal Performance by a Group and also won Song of the Year for Michael and Lionel. Quincy also collected his customary Producer of the Year on the back of it too.

CHAPTER EIGHT

CAN'T BUY ME LOVE

I n May 1985, Michael received a royalty cheque from
CBS Records for $55 million, one of the largest such
cheques in history, but reflective of how successful
Thriller had been. Already rich beyond his wildest
expectations, Michael expected to receive future royalties
of equal if not better amounts for his future recordings,
but something he had heard from Paul McCartney some
months earlier had formulated a plan in his mind.

As a youngster growing up, Michael had been a quick
learner, at least where music matters were concerned.
He had spent countless hours stood in the wings of stages
watching his idols, observing how they handled audiences,
how they moved across the stage. If there was something
that worked particularly well for them, Michael would
practice it and introduce it into his show, and hope it
worked equally well for him. Michael developed much the
same manner in business; look and see what others were
doing and adopt the same kind of plan for himself.

It was while recording 'The Girl Is Mine' that Michael
developed something of a friendship with Paul McCartney
and his wife Linda. During one visit to Paul's country
retreat, Michael listened intently over dinner as Paul
explained how much of his income was derived not from
the sales of his own records but from radio play of others
– over the years Paul had built up an extensive catalogue
of publishing rights that he owned, including just about
everything that Buddy Holly ever wrote. Indeed, Paul had
been such a fan of Buddy Holly that when he first acquired
the publishing rights he had set in motion a stage show and

The Jackson Five photographed in 1968.
Front row: Michael Jackson; middle row:
Tito Jackson, Marlon Jackson, Jermaine
Jackson; back row: Jackie Jackson
(Michael Ochs Archives/Corbis)

Michael Jackson performing in Kansas City,
Kansas, July 1984 during the Victory tour.
(Wally McNamee/Corbis)

Michael Jackson at a news conference in the late 1980s. In spite of the injuries he received when his hair caught fire while filming a Pepsi commercial, Jackson continued to appear in Pepsi adverts throughout the 1980s. (Gary Gershoff/Retna/Corbis)

Lisa-Marie Presley and Michael photographed in January 1995, after their marriage in May 1994. (Corbis Sygma)

Performing in Berlin, August 1997, during the HIStory World Tour (Karl Mittenzwei/epa/Corbis)

CHANGING FACE OF A STAR: Michael on the cover of (clockwise from top left) The Jackson 5's *Greatest Hits* (1971), *Thriller* (1982), *Bad* (1987), and *Off The Wall* (1979).

KING OF POP
MICHAEL JACKSON
THIS IS IT

A press conference at London's O2 Arena 5 March 2009 to announce a 'final show of performances' in July. 'This is it. This is the final curtain call. See you in July.' (STR/epa/Corbis)

musical and almost single-handedly launched a revival of interest in Buddy Holly. Of course, every play on the radio and sale of an album added to Paul's already impressive bank account.

During the course of the dinner Michael got something of a crash course in publishing and how owning copyrights was all important. This had been pretty much the reasoning behind his and his brothers departure from Motown. Berry Gordy wouldn't even allow the brothers to record their own material for inclusion on the B-side (owing to the complexities of the music business, the royalties on singles are split 50/50 between the A and B-sides, irrespective of the fact that most purchasers are only interested in what is on the A side), so Joseph had shopped around for a company that would allow them to share in the royalty income. At some point, however, Paul divulged a simple fact that would prove to be the costliest slip of his life – a deal he and John had signed back in 1964, at the behest of manager Brian Epstein, had cost them 50% of their own future publishing income. The deal they had signed had been with Dick James for the creation of Northern Songs, a company which John and Paul supposedly owned 50% of, but when Dick James came to sell his share, he had sold it on to Sir Lew Grade's ATV Publishing Company rather than sell it back to John and Paul. The ongoing battles between Paul and John's widow Yoko One had meant they had never presented a united front in trying to re-acquire their own copyrights. So now, any time Paul wanted to perform 'Can't Buy Me Love' or 'I Want To Hold You Hand' or any of The Beatles' major hits, he had to pay!

Michael had been an eager listener all evening,

and as he left the couple he said quite simply 'Maybe some day I'll buy your songs.' Paul thought Michael was joking and laughed at the comment, but Michael was deadly serious. If the chance came to buy the catalogue he would pay whatever it cost.

When he returned to America Michael instructed John Branca to search for catalogues of copyrights that he could buy. His first such purchase was of the Sly Stone catalogue. The Jackson 5 had often performed such numbers as 'Stand' during their early days on the road, and now Michael owned the rights. There were a number of other, smaller purchases over the coming months, but it wasn't until September 1984 that word came out that ATV Music might be up for sale. It took Michael some time to realise the importance of the name ATV when John Branca mentioned the potential sale, but when it became obvious that the catalogue included the rights to some 251 John Lennon and Paul McCartney compositions, Michael instructed Branca to pursue the purchase, irrespective of the cost.

The purchase would take eight months to come to fruition. Since Branca knew word would quickly get back to Paul McCartney that one potential buyer was Michael Jackson, he pre-empted the matter by telephoning Linda's father (Paul's father-in-law) John Eastman to ask if Paul intended bidding. The initial reaction was that Paul felt the deal was too expensive, so Branca carried on with his own negotiations to purchase the company. By the time Paul realised that Michael had been serious about buying ATV and tried to get Yoko to link with him in a combined bid, it was too late – on 14 August 1985 Michael Jackson became the new owner of the ATV Publishing Company after paying $47.5 million.

While Michael would not be involved in the day to day running of his newly acquired company, he did give instructions that income had to be maximised; over the next few months Beatles tracks turned up in the unlikeliest of places, including commercials for Nike and Panasonic. Michael would earn a fortune out of each and every deal; Paul would earn only what his contract signed in 1964 stipulated he would earn! Not surprisingly, Paul became extremely bitter towards Michael, feeling he had effectively used inside information in order to buy the company. Paul said at the time 'I think it's dodgy to do things like that. To be someone's friend and then buy the rug they're standing on.' Even an attempt by Paul to get the rates that he earned up nearer to the norm for 1985, rather than the rate that had been fixed in 1964, fell on deaf ears. As far as Michael was concerned, Paul had had two chances to buy his own copyrights back and has passed on them because he thought they were over-priced. It wasn't personal – it was business.

And business for Michael continued to get better. In May 1986 he would sign another deal with Pepsi that would net him $15 million for doing two further commercials and sponsorship for a planned world solo tour. Meanwhile, with *Thriller* continuing to sell there was little pressure on Michael to back into the studio to start working on a follow-up, although he was writing songs at a phenomenal rate so as to ensure he had the material on hand when he was required in the studio. In the meantime, about the only new project Michael was involved with was the production of a 15-minute 3D fantasy film *Captain Eo*, made especially for the Disney company and produced by George Lucas. This would take nearly a year to complete, during which time Disney built a special theatre in both their Disneyland (California) and Disneyworld (Florida) complexes in order to show the finished article, which reportedly cost some $20 million to produce.

Michael and Quincy did work on material for the *Captain Eo* project, 'Another Part Of Me', which would eventually be included on the next solo album *Bad*. While recording may not have started on the album, planning had. Michael had in mind doing an album that would be a series of duets, featuring some of the biggest names in music, and he instructed Frank Dileo and to a lesser extent John Branca to sound out some of the artists Michael expressed an interest in working with. One of the first to be approached was Prince, an artist who had come out of nowhere at the start of the decade and had become a serious rival to Michael. So serious, in fact, that Michael was reluctant to consider working with Prince when it was first suggested, not least because as far as Michael was concerned, they were the complete opposite – at least as far as they were perceived by their respective audiences. Eventually, Michael overcame his reluctance and a meeting was arranged between the pair. It turned out to be a complete disaster: neither wanted to give anything away so they sat and stared at each other for most of the time! When the matter of recording together was mentioned to Prince, he said he would consider it depending on the song that was on offer; when he heard 'Bad' he said the project wasn't for him, although the word that got back to Michael was that Prince had turned it down because he felt it would be a hit without Prince's contribution. This was especially disappointing for Michael, for in addition to the song he also had in mind a campaign that would turn the track into a surefire smash – he would have his team put out a number of derogatory stories about Prince, and

Prince's people would retaliate with stories about Michael, thus building up a feeling of deep resentment between the two artists within the media. Then the joint single would appear and the media would realise they had been taken in by both camps. Later Prince would state he turned down the suggestion the first time he heard the first line of the song, 'Your butt is mine.' 'I ain't saying that to you, and you sure ain't saying that to me' was his response!

Others proved equally elusive. 'I Just Can't Stop Loving You' was originally considered as a duet for Michael and Barbra Streisand, but Streisand turned the collaboration down because of the disparity in their ages. The thought of a 44-year-old woman and a 29-year-old man singing a homage to each other didn't seem right to her. The idea was similarly rejected by others approached by or on behalf of Michael, including Whitney Houston and Aretha Franklin. Perhaps the only female singer who *might* have considered it to be right was Madonna, but Michael didn't think much of her, either as an artist or as a person. The new album, therefore, would have to be done as another solo effort.

CHAPTER NINE
WHO'S BAD?

Michael had begun writing and recording demos for what would become the *Bad* album soon after the Victory tour had been completed. In all he had about 60 new songs ready for consideration, and Quincy had again asked for contributions from others for possible inclusion.

With his plans for a duets album scrapped, Michael now pondered whether he should do all the songs he had available, and make the new release a triple album. Quincy would eventually talk him out of this plan, reasoning that it would be better to do a single album that contained the strongest songs, rather than release something that had variable quality. He did, however, agree to record some 30 tracks in all and then decide at a later date which were the strongest ones to include.

If the disagreements between Michael and Quincy had made the recording of *Thriller* at times difficult, they were nothing compared with those that accompanied the sessions for *Bad*. As the artist behind the creation of the best-selling album in the world, Michael felt his voice should carry the most weight around the studio, and what he said went as far as the selection of material and how the final sound was accomplished were concerned. Quincy was not trying to interfere in such matters, merely point out to Michael – with the benefit of his considerable years of experience – that *together* they were trying to create an album that would stand comparison with its predecessor. It did not help matters that Michael had pinned up a note that simply stated '100 million' – the number of copies of *Bad* he expected to sell. This was a move seemingly designed solely to place additional pressure on all concerned.

Recording of the album commenced in August 1986, with Quincy's view that they should concentrate on the best songs Michael had written finally winning through. This meant that, of the 11 tracks that would eventually make it on to *Bad*, Michael had written nine. The remaining two tracks came from the pens of Terry Britton and Graham Lyle, who contributed 'Just Good Friends', which Michael recorded as a duet with Stevie Wonder, and Glen Ballard and Siedah Garrett, who wrote 'Man In The Mirror', a song that would become something of an anthem. As well as an accomplished writer, Siedah was also an exceptionally good singer – good enough, in fact, for Quincy to suggest that 'I Just Can't Stop Loving You' could be done as a duet between Michael and Siedah.

There was continued debate between Michael and Quincy throughout the sessions regarding the songs that would eventually appear on the album. One such disagreement concerned the tracks 'Streetwalker' and 'Another Part Of Me'. Michael liked the former and thought it should appear, a point of view that Quincy disagreed with. Fortunately for Quincy, he found something of an ally in Frank Dileo, who danced in the studio whenever 'Another Part Of Me' was played but didn't when 'Streetwalker' was played – 'Another Part Of Me' made it onto the finished album, 'Streetwalker' didn't. Michael, however, would get his own way with 'Smooth Criminal', another song Quincy was unsure about.

One thing was for sure; 'Bad' might not be recorded as a duet but it certainly was going to be single at some point, and Michael wanted the accompanying video to surpass anything he had previously produced. To this end he hired Martin Scorsese to direct at various locations in the Bronx, with the storyline to the video being centred on the real life story of Edmund Perry, a student shot to death by a plainclothes policeman in June 1985. The finished article again contains many references to *West Side Story*, which Michael had first visited with the video to 'Beat It'.

Michael then produced video clips for 'The Way You Make Me Feel' and 'Smooth Criminal', eventually spending an unprecedented $40 million on video production alone! John Branca would eventually put together a deal with CBS that would see all of the clips released as a compilation, for which Michael received an advance of $30 million, thus clawing back a significant part of the outlay.

One of the only tracks for which a video *wasn't* produced was 'I Just Can't Stop Loving You', which was released as the lead single on 20 July 1987. While work was still continuing on finishing the album, Michael had decided to release the single as something as a taster for what was to come, similar to the campaign for *Thriller*. For the best part of a year, all manner of stories had been appearing in the media about Michael. Among the most memorable were the story that he slept in an oxygen chamber so that he might live to be 150, and the rumour that he was trying to buy the remains of John 'Elephant Man' Merrick. Both these stories, and plenty more besides, were planted by Michael and his team, the intention being to ensure continued interest in the star. The plan would eventually backfire: since half the stories that were submitted or planted were totally unbelievable or made Michael out to be some kind of freak, some sections of the media started making up their own equally unbelievable stories about him. While Michael was in control of what was being said, the focus was on maintaining a presence in the media in advance of his new material. To this end, 'I Just Can't Stop Loving You' was assured everyone's attention when it was finally released to radio.

While 'I Just Can't Stop Loving You' began its climb up the chart, Michael and Walter Yetnikoff worked on a plan to get the heads of the major retail outlets on their side from the start. Michael extended an invitation in July to the lucky heads to join him at his home in Encino to listen to the new album, which was by then just about ready for release and had been slated to hit the streets on 31 August. For once Michael involved his family in the campaign, with the 50 or retail heads being largely entertained on the day by LaToya and Joseph at the family home Hayvenhurst. Michael himself made only a fleeting appearance to pose for photographs, citing his shyness as a reason for him not being more actively involved in the day's proceedings.

While retail prepared themselves for the impending release of the album, CBS around the world worked on the single 'I Just Can't Stop Loving You' (interestingly, although the single was performed as a duet, Siedah Garrett did not receive a credit). A Spanish language version, translated and co-produced by Ruben Blades as 'Todo Mi Amor Eres Tu' would aid sales in certain sections of the market, but in truth the demand for new Michael Jackson material had already assured the single of a positive reception. It debuted at #5 on the UK charts and hit number one a week later, where it would remain for two weeks. In the US it was to spend only one week at the summit but would go on to earn a gold disc for sales of half a million copies – the campaign for the album was off to a positive start.

Despite the success of the first single, however, Michael was concerned. Expectations were high, both within his own camp and at CBS, further adding to the pressure on the album to deliver. To this end, Michael produced a commemorative film *The Magic Returns* that was aired on CBS on the day of release, 31 August. At the end of the special, the full, 17-minute long video of 'Bad' was screened. There was also news that a tour, imaginatively titled The Bad Tour would kick off in Tokyo in September, the first date in a virtual around the world extravaganza that would eventually become the highest grossing tour up to that point, even if a number of dates were cancelled owing to poor ticket sales! With an elaborate marketing plan also in place, it was obvious that Michael and his team would be pushing *Bad* for all it was worth in an effort to surpass *Thriller*.

Always a major fan base, Britain took to the album even more than they had *Thriller*. It entered the chart at number one and would stay there for five weeks during its 125 week run on the charts over the next few years. Most surprisingly, it would ultimately sell *more* copies than *Thriller* during that time – *Thriller* had earned 11 multi-platinum awards, *Bad* topped it with 13 on its way to selling 3.9 million copies (only one album, Oasis's *Morning Glory* has achieved higher sales status).

Both the UK and US went with 'Bad' as the follow-up single, with the already aired video adding to the promotional push. A #3 hit in the UK, the single made it all the way to the top in the US and enjoyed a two week stay at the summit. The third single, the punchy 'The Way You Make Me Feel' repeated its positioning on both sides of the Atlantic; #3 UK and #1 US. Then came 'Man In The Mirror', the song written by Siedah Garrett and featuring the Winans and the Andre Crouch Choir on backing vocals. Although often regarded as one of his best-known songs among his British fans, the single limped to #21 on its initial release (although it would surge back to #2 in the aftermath of Michael's death some 22 years later). In the US it returned Michael to the top of the charts and also spent two weeks looking down at the competition. 'Dirty Diana' was then released as the fifth single and became his fifth consecutive US number one – as well as returning him to the upper reaches of the UK chart, where it hit #4.

Just as they had done with *Thriller* earlier, both CBS and Michael continued pulling additional tracks off the *Bad* album for release as singles; 'Another Part Of Me' only just missed the Top Ten in the US, peaking at #11 (it made #15 in the UK) and 'Smooth Criminal' made the Top Ten on either side of the Atlantic, peaking at #7 in the US and #8 in the UK. In the UK there was yet another single release, with 'Liberian Girl' making #13 in June 1989, nearly *two years* after the album had first appeared on the market!

Perhaps it was because *Thriller* was such a monumental hit that *Bad* has tended to be overshadowed. While *Thriller* had sold over 28 million copies in the US alone, *Bad* barely made 8 million, meaning the album is viewed as something of a failure in that territory. Yet no other artist in history had managed to lift five consecutive number ones from the same album, and the final tally of six Top Ten hits had only been surpassed by his own success earlier.

All told, *Bad* would sell some 30 million copies worldwide – a figure that surpassed anything any of his contemporaries were capable of, but which fell well short of Michael's hopes and expectations. There would be several high-level meetings and discussions analysing the

perceived 'failure' of the album, with Michael and
his team largely laying the blame at the door of CBS.
Yet the album got every possible assistance from the
record company, as the tally of five number ones would
confirm. Similarly, Michael's extravagant expenditure on
the videos for the singles had certainly assured maximum
publicity and plays across all forms of the media, so it
wasn't for lack of exposure that the album failed to hit the
same kind of sales plateau as its predecessor. Perhaps, in
the final analysis, both parties should have accepted what
many reviewers said at the time of release; it just wasn't
as good an album as *Thriller*. Of course *Thriller* had also
been dismissed in certain quarters as not being a patch on
his earlier effort *Off The Wall*, but had gone on to prove
its worth over time. *Thriller* had effectively come out of
nowhere in terms of sales. No one expected it to do as well
as it had - all concerned were pleasantly surprised when it
went into sales overdrive. Yet *Bad* had been expected to
hit the ground running, a record-busting phenomenon right
from day one – and musical history has shown that nearly
every artist has struggled to maintain or better their sales
at some point in their careers. It had happened to Bruce
Springsteen after *Born In The USA*, The Beatles after
Sgt Pepper and Prince after *Purple Rain*. Michael Jackson
might have thought he was different from every other artist
in the world, both past and present, but really he was as
susceptible to changing buying patterns as anyone else.

The post-mortem that Michael and his team conducted
also identified other reasons for the album's relative
failure. *Thriller* had been honoured with collecting a total
of 12 nominations for Grammy Awards and walked off
with eight of them (seven for Michael, one of which was
shared with Quincy, and the engineering award to Bruce

Swedien), the virtual clean sweep he achieved resulting in yet another sales surge for the album. By comparison, *Bad* had garnered a rather more modest four nominations, although this was sufficient for Michael to accept an invitation to attend the awards. Not only that, but Michael also agreed to perform at the ceremony, held at the Radio City Hall in New York, singing 'The Way You Make Me Feel' and 'Man In The Mirror'. He received rapturous applause and acclaim for his performance, but it turned out to be the only applause he got all night – he was beaten in all four categories. Of the four, his defeat in the Album of the Year category by U2 and their album *The Joshua Tree* hurt most, for while he may have sold more albums than former Motown labelmate Stevie Wonder, he had still not come anywhere close to matching his record at the Grammy's, where Stevie had won the Album of the Year award three times in four years. The only year he didn't win was the year he hadn't released an album, a fact that had been duly noted and praised by that year's winner Paul Simon!

Having been feted by his peers in 1984, was he now being punished for not having presented the right image over the previous year or so? This was certainly a consideration: had the Academy deliberately avoided voting for a man that was now known as 'Wacko Jacko' as far as some sections of the media were concerned? If so, then Michael had no one else to blame but himself. The planting of stories about oxygen chambers and buying the Elephant Man's remains might have seemed like a good idea at the time, but the media was now having a field day at his expense planting their own stories. Aside from supposedly having considered marriage to a number of women, including Katherine Hepburn (none of which were true), the rivalry between Michael and Prince had supposedly escalated, with Prince using ESP in order to send Michael's pet chimp Bubbles mad! The story was totally preposterous, of course, and even Michael had a good chuckle when he saw it in print for the first time. But the damage was done, because the reading public had no way of knowing which stories were true and which were not.

CHAPTER TEN

LEAVE ME ALONE

Michael and his management inner circle weren't the only ones concerned about the way his image was being portrayed. His family, in particular his mother Katherine, were becoming horrified by the way he was being represented in the media. Katherine felt sure that Frank Dileo was the man responsible for her son being viewed so negatively, but when she got no joy from trying to talk to him, she turned her attentions to Michael himself, frequently quizzing him on why he was allowing himself to be so manipulated. Katherine got even less joy from Michael, and he found himself going out of his way to avoid her and the rest of the family. He had already planned on moving out of Hayvenhurst (he had bought the majority share in the house from his parents a few years previously but had remained living there) and had found a property that he liked, set in a 2700 acre estate in the Santa Ynez Valley.

Then known as Sycamore Ranch, Michael had first come across the property when he and Paul McCartney had filmed the video to 'Say Say Say', with Paul and Linda having leased the home while they were staying in America. As luck would have it, Michael soon learned that the owner, developer William Bone, was looking to offload the property and had put a price of $32.5 million on it (although if the eventual purchaser wanted to keep all of the furniture, the price would rise to $35 million). Those close to Michael, including John Branca, who would have to do all of the negotiating, felt the price was way too high – even given the type of wealth that Michael had accumulated in such a short space of time. Branca's main concern was that there would be no profit should Michael think about selling it in the future: the price was so high that only the maker of the best-selling album in the world could consider making such a purchase! Michael wasn't particularly concerned about the resale value, rather the fact that it had room enough to allow him to indulge in all his passions, including the creation of a menagerie. Even more importantly, the location put sufficient distance between him and the rest of his family. He therefore instructed John Branca to make an initial offer of 50% of the asking price; the final sum eventually handed over was nearer $28 million.

Soon after taking ownership of the property, Michael changed its name to Neverland Valley, in homage to the JJ Barrie story *Peter Pan*. Michael had always stated in interviews that he had felt he had missed out on his childhood, thanks to the demands of being a pop star – so if he was the boy who never grew up then what better name could there be? Michael wasted little time in turning the property into his own dreamland. 'Because I wanted to have a place where I could create everything that I never had as a child. So, you see rides. You see animals. There's a movie theater. Everything that I love is behind those gates. We have elephants, and giraffes, and crocodiles, and every kind of tigers and lions. And – and we have bus loads of kids, who don't get to see those things. They come up sick children, and enjoy it.'

That comment about helping sick children probably summed up the real Michael Jackson at that time. While the media was portraying him as Wacko Jacko, the caring Michael Jackson was donating vast sums of money to charities around the world. On the day after the Grammy

Awards debacle, Michael had handed over a cheque for $600,000, his entire proceeds from a concert at Madison Square, to the United Negro College Fund. Almost everywhere he went, Michael would find out which were the local charities, especially those concerned with sick children, and make vast anonymous donations. Therein lay the problem, in a sense: if the media had known the kind of money Michael was handing over, perhaps they might not have given him such a rough ride over other aspects of his life. Then again, knowing Michael's luck, maybe one or two would have reported it as Michael donating such money in order to generate good publicity – he just couldn't win whatever he did.

Michael had conducted the purchase of Neverland Valley as a cloak and dagger operation, for while there was little likelihood that he was going to be gazumped in buying the property, he did not want the rest of the family aware of his future plans. He knew, with good reason, that they would try and turn him away from not only buying that particular property, but any other that might take his fancy. Joseph may have long ceased being his manager, but there were still frequent requests from Michael to consider himself a member of the Jackson family and undertake some tour or some recording that would benefit them all. And that was now the last thing on Michael's mind. As it happened, the negotiations and eventual purchase were conducted secretly, so the first the rest of the Jackson family knew of his impending departure was when they saw it on *Entertainment News* after the event! Even then they tried to convince him to return home. In retaliation, when Michael held a house-warming party a few weeks later, Joseph and Katherine Jackson were conspicuous by their absence, for Michael omitted to invite them.

If the release of *Bad* had been supposedly mistimed, then Michael's departure from the family home, at the age of 33 years, was as well-timed as any other event in his life. While Michael was instructing his assorted aids to return to the home in Encino and remove his affects from his room, Joseph and his then president of business affairs Jerome Howard had entered into discussions with a Korean frontman, Kenneth Choi. The plan was simple enough. For a considerably large sum of money, the Koreans wanted the Jacksons to tour their country. There was only one proviso, of course: Michael Jackson had to be a part of the tour. Michael had stated after the Victory tour that he did not intend touring with his brothers ever again, but Joseph and the rest of the Jackson brothers had not made the kind of money from that tour that had enabled *them* to put away their instruments for some time yet.

There was only one thing Michael was willing to put his name to at the time; his autobiography. In October 1983 Michael had met with the former First Lady Jackie Kennedy Onassis to discuss writing an autobiography to be published by Doubleday, where Jackie was a senior editor. The pair had first met a few years earlier, when Michael had been filming *The Wiz* in New York, and Jackie would eventually become a member of Michael's inner circle of friends. An initial manuscript of the 'autobiography', to be called *Moonwalk,* was written by Robert Hillburn, but was rejected by Doubleday as it was not 'juicy' enough. A second manuscript was then written by Stephen Davis and given to Michael to look over and verify. Horrified by what he read, Michael drastically edited it but then realised that the only way to get the story he wanted was for him to actually write the book himself. He hired Share Areheart to assist him in writing the book, although she would leave the project before it was completed (according to certain rumours she left after Michael threw a snake at her!) The finished manuscript was then sent to Jackie Kennedy Onassis to be edited and for her to write a three paragraph introduction.

The whole project was conducted amidst the tightest of security. Employees of Doubleday and their relatives were used to deliver the completed manuscript from the head office in Manhattan to the printing plant in Pennsylvania, where the book was given the code name 'Neil Armstrong', the very first moonwalker. In all the book took some four years to write, finally appearing in May 1988.

Although when published the book was widely received as being a watered-down version of the Michael Jackson story, there was still sufficient interest to send it to the top of the bestseller lists inside the first week. *Moonwalk* would eventually sell nearly half a million copies inside the first couple of months from publication, proof that there was still enormous interest in Michael's story. Michael used the book to both confirm and dispel a number of myths about himself. Yes, he had had surgery on his face – two operations on his nose and the creation of a cleft in his chin. He also attributed the overall change in his face structure to a number of other factors; puberty, weight loss, his vegetarian diet. A change in hair style and stage lighting had radically changed the way he looked. The book also detailed the strict upbringing and the beatings he had suffered at the hands of his father, with the result that Michael thought of himself as one of the loneliest people in the world.

The success of the book was replicated by the release of a film entitled *Moonwalker,* which featured live footage from his shows, music videos and a feature film starring Michael and Joe Pesci. Initially released in film theatres in Japan, its subsequent issue on video would become another major success, topping the Billboard Music Video Cassette chart for 22 weeks before it was finally dethroned by the release of *Michael Jackson: The Legend Continues.*

While the autobiography was not ultimately the juicy exposé that Doubleday had hoped for, there were still elements within it that troubled Michael, in particular the negative way his father was portrayed. In an attempt to defuse the atmosphere between himself and his father, Michael telephoned Joseph while on tour in the UK and apologised for some of the content, claiming that he had not been responsible for writing the whole book and that anything that appeared to be critical was written by someone else! Joseph accepted the apology – not least because he had a pressing need to get back into Michael's good books, owing to a growing number of financial problems he was having. Joseph had recently lost nearly a million dollars on a failed oil well investment and the collapse of his own beverage company, and had also had a judgement entered against him after writing out a cheque for $7.1 million that had subsequently been returned unpaid. The judgement was for a further $3 million dollars, a sum of money which only Michael had instant access to, but since Michael had effectively distanced himself from his family he had no intention of further helping his father.

If Michael wouldn't help his father directly, then there had to be another way of securing sufficient funds indirectly, with a reunion tour of all the brothers in Korea offering the kind of financial salvation that Joseph needed.

Joseph called a family conference while Michael was on the Japanese leg of his Bad tour, in order to get the rest of the family on side – he would turn his attentions to Michael later. The family meeting, however, did not go as well as Joseph had hoped, with Marlon refusing to have anything to do with such a tour. He too had felt the Victory tour had been a step too far and would not agree to sign up for this latest Jackson money-making scheme. The rest of the brothers were all up for it, however, even hoping that they might be able to do the tour without Michael if he couldn't be persuaded to join. Joseph at this time knew that the money being put up for the tour was ultimately coming from the Moonies and that the megabucks on offer were conditional on Michael being a part of it. Besides, the chances of the Jacksons being able to fill the 60,000 stadium earmarked for the Seoul dates were too slim to contemplate.

Michael's *Bad* tour finally came to a close at the Los Angeles Memorial Coliseum & Sports Arena in January 1989, with five sell-out dates. A total of 4.5 million people had seen the tour that had commenced in September 1987, with ticket sales having generated $125 million. Michael's initial plan was to head off to Neverland with his friend Jimmy Safechuck in order to recuperate after what had been a gruelling trek around the world. Jimmy had been a travelling companion throughout the tour, sometimes in the company of his parents, sometimes alone, but the friendship and how it was perceived had begun to perplex Frank Dileo. Jimmy was just ten years old when he first linked up with the tour, where Michael arranged to have specially made uniforms similar to his own for the youngster to wear. He also gave a gift of a Rolls Royce car costing a hundred thousand dollars to Jimmy's parents, an act that Dileo also felt would be misconstrued. Whenever Dileo tried to raise the delicate matter with Michael, he would be angrily rebuffed – Michael saw nothing wrong in his friendship with the youngster, on whom he lavished thousand of dollars of gifts and presents, and it was no one's business but his.

While Michael's friendships with a succession of youngsters were not yet public news, an equally damming story was about to break over which Michael had little or no control. Like the rest of the Jackson children, LaToya had sacked her father as her manager and taken up with Jack Gordon, an older man who she would later marry. LaToya's recording career was never spectacular but she obviously needed to generate her own income. Depending on the sources, she was either coerced or enthusiastically agreed to do a photo session for *Playboy* magazine. When this news reached Michael it sent him into something of a rage, as it went completely against the wholesome image the Jacksons had spent a lifetime cultivating. Michael spoke directly to *Playboy* boss Hugh Hefner, and extracted an agreement that Michael would get to see the pictures before anyone else, once they had been retouched. The pictures were duly sent to Michael, who presumably tried to get the article and pictures pulled from the magazine, but whatever it was that he offered, it did not have the desired affect. Eleven pictures of LaToya Jackson naked duly appeared in *Playboy* magazine. To make matters even worse, LaToya then appeared on television to state that Michael had actually approved the pictures! Michael spoke to his mother and had a long conversation about the matter, the upshot being that he effectively cut his sister out of his life, changing his telephone number and instructing that no one was to give her the number under any circumstances.

His only comment on the subject was 'I can't control her, just as they can't control me. So, good for her, I guess. She did what she had to do and she didn't care about any of us, did she? When I do that kind of thing, they all come down on me, hard. So, good for her if she can take it. Good for her.' Thereafter the Michael Jackson entourage were expressly forbidden to mention the photo session ever again.

The fact that Michael had tried to intervene before the pictures appeared in *Playboy* was proof, at least as far as Joseph Jackson saw it, that Michael still cared for his family. Therefore, if he could be made aware of the financial situation the rest of the family was in he could be persuaded to agree to the Korean deal. To try and speed matters along, the Koreans put something of a bounty on Michael's head – any member of the family or entourage that got Michael's signature on the contract would be guaranteed an immediate payment of $1 million. Previously reluctant to ask Michael directly whether he would commit to the dates, now all of the family was trying to get his attention. Michael had no intention of rejoining his brothers for one last tour, mainly because he knew it would not be the last – there would be other requests in the future. So while his mother Katherine tried the softly-softly approach to try to get him aboard, Joseph tried verbally bullying him. Such actions may have worked in the past; now they stood little chance of succeeding. Irrespective of the financial rewards on offer, Michael Jackson would not join with his brothers in Korea. Or anywhere else for that matter. As far as Michael was concerned, the subject was now a closed one.

With Joseph Jackson's business empire teetering on the brink of collapse, Jerome Howard tried a different route to getting Michael to at least consider the tour – he paid for

an introduction to Frank Dileo. At the resultant meeting,
Kenneth Choi revealed that he had two cheques for half
a million dollars each, both of which would be made
out to Dileo in return for getting Michael's agreement to
undertake the Korean tour. Dileo informed the pair that the
final decision on whether Michael toured Korea would be
for Michael to make, irrespective of the money that was
on offer to Frank for him to get Michael's agreement. He
would, however, talk to Michael about the tour. Other than
that he could promise nothing.

Frank did sit down with Michael to discuss the proposed
tour and quickly sensed that Michael was dead set against
linking up with his brothers. Rather than push the point,
Frank asked Michael to think it over and let him know
the outcome. Three days later came the bombshell. A
statement issued by Michael's publicist read 'Michael
Jackson and Frank Dileo have announced an amicable
parting. Jackson said "I thank Frank for his contribution on
my behalf during the past several years."' Frank himself
was informed of the decision by John Branca, who had
been instructed by Michael to convey his decision.

While the approach by Frank to Michael on the Korean
tour may have been the catalyst to their parting, the reality
was that it had been on the cards for at least a year, with
Frank possibly being the architect of his own demise.
Michael had expressed to others within his entourage
that he felt Frank was getting too much of the credit for
his success. It had not helped that Frank was invariably
featured in the media, talking about various aspects of
Michael's career, but this was largely because Michael
was not doing interviews at this time. It was better for the
media to have access to at least one highly-placed member
of the team than none at all. The release of *Moonwalker*

had also caused friction between the pair, with Michael
blaming Frank for not getting the film released in theatres
in the US, a decision that reportedly cost Michael millions
in lost revenue. However, Frank had come up with a
contingency plan whereby a multimillion dollar offer
was put on the table for domestic distribution, only for
Michael to veto the decision. Perhaps the most vital aspect
of Michael's decision to sever ties with Frank Dileo was
the continued negative publicity Michael was attracting
in certain sections of the media, with the 'Wacko Jacko'
moniker showing no sign of disappearing. While Michael
had concocted many of the earlier stories, including the
oxygen chamber, Frank had been an eager participant and
had subsequently come up with his own, equally bizarre
stories. When stories continued to appear even after
Michael had ordered his team to stop feeding the media,
he suspected Frank Dileo as being the man responsible.

With Frank Dileo no longer an influential figure
in the Michael Jackson camp, Joseph Jackson and
Jerome Howard were in something of a panic, for there
appeared to be no one they could approach to attempt
to get Michael's ear. A conversation with Michael's
accountant offered a glimmer of hope, if only because
as an accountant he was looking to maximise Michael's
revenue streams. He suggested speaking to John Branca,
who had effectively moved up the pecking order within
the entourage. In the event, it was a combination of
Joseph and Katherine Jackson together with Kenneth
Choi who persuaded Michael to reconsider his decision.
An opportune call by Michael to Hayvenhurst on a day
Choi happened to be discussing strategy with Joseph and
Katherine resulted in Choi having a brief conversation
with Michael, at which he extracted an agreement to meet

and outline the plans. The meeting duly took place and eventually, after a total of six months behind-the-scenes activity, Michael signed a contract to appear in Korea for four shows in August. The sums of money had reached astronomical proportions, with Michael being guaranteed $8 million for his part in the show – a total of four solo songs and a medley of hits with his brothers, while the rest of the show would be done by the other Jackson brothers, not Michael.

It would appear that the constant requests had effectively worn down Michael's resolve not to do the shows, for by the time he realised what he had signed up for and asked John Branca to investigate, the tour was a done deal. Except that it wasn't quite: if John Branca had been asked to try to get Michael out of the contract, others had already set those wheels in motion, with the Reverend Moon feeling that the figures that had been agreed were too high even for his resources. Thus Michael received a revised offer to perform for just $7 million, then $5 million and further on downwards, until the money on offer became a rather derisory $2.5 million. Then the deal collapsed altogether, with the Reverend Moon and his Segye Times Inc company suing Michael for the return for various gifts and financial sweeteners that had been paid to try and get the deal in the first place. Michael subsequently counter-sued, stating he had no intention of handing back the Rolls Royce or any of the other gifts and he doubted the rest of his family (the others named in the original suit were Joseph Jackson, Katherine Jackson, Jermaine Jackson, Jerome Howard and Bill Bray, Michael's security manager) and confidants would hand back theirs. As the deal finally collapsed, Michael said 'I don't even know how this whole thing happened, or how I got involved in it.

All I know is that I kept saying no, no, no. But my family would not take no for an answer. Look what happened as a result. The whole thing made me sick. Just sick.'

Then it was LaToya's turn to once again cause her brother discomfort, this time with the news that she was planning on writing her autobiography. While LaToya writing about her own life did not appear to be a cause for concern, the *Playboy* photo shoot notwithstanding, the news that she would reveal that Michael had been sexually abused as a child undoubtedly was – no doubt the rumour of what LaToya intended revealing was sufficient to get her a $500,000 advance from Putnam publishing house, some $200,000 more than Michael had received for his own autobiography from Doubleday! Enraged, Michael instructed John Branca to speak to Jack Gordon and ascertain exactly what was going to be said in the book. While rumours of Michael having been molested had circulated around the industry for years, Michael had always strenuously denied them and that had been the end of the matter. Now that a family member was threatening to go public with the rumours, it was time to nip this particular story in the bud. Branca met with Gordon and firmly stated that Michael would sue LaToya if she wrote about the molestation rumours.

If Michael was enraged enough to threaten to sue, Jack Gordon thought he saw a way of making additional money from the proposed autobiography. Through an intermediary he suggested that the autobiography would be cancelled if Joseph and Katherine paid $5 million, money they obviously didn't have. Then stories started reaching the media that Michael was offering $12 million for the book to be cancelled and finally that he had bid $84 million in order to buy GP Putnam! Neither story was true, for Michael had said 'She doesn't get a free ride just by saying Jack is the one doing the dirty work. She has to take responsibility, just like I do. I'm not going to let my own sister, a person I loved, a person who has known me all my life, blackmail me. This is as low as you can go. Tell LaToya I said she can go jump in a lake. She's not getting one dime from me.'

When the book, entitled *La Toya: Growing Up In The Jackson Family*, finally appeared in 1991, there were no such revelations about Michael. If anything the book was a mere retread of Michael's own story, with Joseph being further castigated for having been abusive towards all of the children as they were growing up.

As if Michael didn't have enough to worry about as the new decade loomed, CBS would soon be expecting a new album to release onto the market. With Michael now manager-less, it fell to John Branca to negotiate with CBS on a new contract. Branca also suggested to Michael that his next album should be a career retrospective, with the provisional title of *Decade* being given to the album. The original plan was for the tapes to be delivered to CBS in August 1989 for release in November, with the plans for such an album sufficient to earn Michael an advance of $18 million, which was made up of a $15 million recoupable against future royalties and a $3 million gift. In addition, there was a $5 million advance from Warner Tamerlane Publishing, the company that administered Michael's music publishing interests worldwide. All told, with guarantees, advances and an improved royalty rate of $2.08 per album, the deal was said to be worth some $50 million in total. Such a deal, therefore, was said to be the largest in recording history, topping previous mega deals for artists such as Billy Joel, Neil Diamond and

Bruce Springsteen. When the deal was finally announced, in March 1991, it topped the previous highest ever deal signed a week earlier by Janet Jackson with Virgin!

Much of the groundwork for the contract was laid by John Branca, whose negotiating skills and business acumen had turned Michael into one of the richest men in the recording industry. Yet by the time Michael signed the contract, John Branca had been given his marching orders in much the same way as Frank Dileo earlier: a letter from Michael's accountant delivered by special messenger informed John Branca that his services were no longer required by Michael Jackson.

Although Michael had a rough idea of the track listing for *Decade,* he had not delivered the tapes to CBS by the end of the year. Instead, on the advice of industry mogul David Geffen, Michael decided the time wasn't right for a retrospective: there was still plenty to say about the current. He would therefore work on delivering a new album to CBS for release in November 1991, with work commencing on the new album in June 1990.

CHAPTER ELEVEN
DANGEROUS

F rank Dileo and John Branca were not the only
departures from the Michael Jackson camp.
Michael had decided that his new album *Dangerous*
needed a new sound and a new producer. Quincy Jones
was therefore cut adrift too. Whereas Branca and Dileo
received written confirmation that they were no longer
needed, no such letter was sent to Quincy Jones. Indeed,
Quincy repeatedly stated right up until Michael's death
in 2009 that he expected to work with his protégé again
at some point. However, the pair did have a number of
conversations about the direction Michael wished to go
with the music for his new album. It was Quincy himself
who suggested that Michael hook up with Teddy Riley and
Bill Bottrell, two of the leading purveyors of the New Jack
Swing sound.

Teddy Riley had been a member of Guy with Aaron
Hall and Timmy Gatling (Gatling was subsequently
replaced by Aaron's brother Damion) and had scored a
number of hits with their first two albums. Riley, however,
was at that point more interested in writing and producing
than performing and had also penned for the likes of
Bobby Brown and Johnny Kemp. At just 22 years of age
and almost ten years younger than Michael, he would be
expected to provide the link into a younger audience for
Michael's music. Bill Bottrell, by contrast, would be the
older, experienced hand guiding the project overall.

The atmosphere within the Ocean Way Studio in Los
Angeles was convivial, which was just as well as the
sessions would ultimately last for some 16 months. This

was not a case of Michael taking deliberately longer recording the album, rather the relatively new medium of the compact disc would mean that more music could fit on than the old vinyl version (*Dangerous* would ultimately be released as a two-disc vinyl album), with the 14 tracks that made the final cut stretching the length of the album to some 77 minutes.

Michael wrote or co-wrote 12 of the tracks, with the remaining two being penned by Teddy Riley and Bernard Belle ('Why You Wanna Trip On Me') and Larry Grossman and Buz Kohan ('Gone Too Soon'). Three of the tracks were written by Michael alone, Teddy Riley contributed to six and three of the tracks would feature raps. The link with Teddy Riley in particular would bring about revised interest in Michael's music from the black market.

Just as he had done with *Bad*, Michael planned and produced a series of stunning videos to accompany the eventual singles that were released. Here in particular his creativity was expanding, for many of the videos would feature celebrity friends in various situations. The first such video ('Black Or White') featured Macauley Culkin (the star of the *Home Alone* film series) and, if you look closely enough during the morphing segment, a young Tyra Banks. This video was directed by John Landis, whose previous work with Michael had included *Thriller.* There was considerable controversy when the ten minute version of 'Black and White' first aired on MTV, with numerous complaints being received over the number of times Michael grabbed his crotch while dancing. Subsequent screenings of the video omitted the final four minutes, deemed to be the most controversial section of the film.

Eddie Murphy and Iman appeared in the video to 'Remember The Time', playing the role of Pharaoh and his wife respectively. The selection of Eddie Murphy perhaps raised the most eyebrows, for Murphy had frequently delivered a quite wicked impersonation of Michael that poked fun at almost every aspect of Michael, his career and life. Murphy's selection at least proved that Michael had a sense of humour! Also featured was basketball player Earvin Johnson, better known as Magic Johnson.

Other stars who made appearances included another basketball player in Michael Jordan in 'Jam' and Naomi Campbell in 'In The Closet'. Campbell may have appeared in the video, but the female singer credited as Mystery Girl on the album was rumoured to be Princess Stephanie of Monaco, although Michael's original intention had been for Madonna to feature. Each successive video stretched the boundaries in much the same way 'Beat It' and 'Thriller' had done almost a decade earlier. 'Black Or White', for example, was one of the earliest examples of computer generated morphing, while the dance routines and special effects in 'Remember The Time' were straight out of Hollywood.

The respective campaigns for the single and album got off to the best possible starts. The single 'Black Or White' entered the UK chart at number one and remained there for two weeks on its way to selling more than a quarter of a million copies. In the US it hit number one inside three weeks and spent seven weeks at the summit, selling more than a million copies and earning Michael a platinum sales award, his first such award since *Thriller*. The appearance of Saul Hudson (better known as Slash of Guns N' Roses) on guitar helped the single become one his most appealing singles across the board since 'Beat It'. The video, which was premiered on Fox, BET and MTV in the US and Top of the Pops in the UK, and its attendant controversy, only helped in the long run.

The campaign for *Dangerous*, meanwhile, kicked off with the kind of incident that had some sections of the media believing Frank Dileo was still orchestrating the publicity campaign. On the eve of release, 30,000 copies of the album were stolen from Los Angeles Airport by three gunmen brandishing shotguns! Despite this shortfall in copies to buy, the album still shifted enough to land quickly at the top of the US charts, where it would spend four weeks. In the UK it had to be content with a single week stay at the summit, but it would rack up nearly two years on the listings. This would tally almost exactly with the singles that were released from the album over the next two years.

In January 1992 came the second single 'Remember The Time', which would hit number three on both sides of the Atlantic. By then plans were well underway for another world tour, which was duly announced at a press conference at Radio City Music Hall in New York on 2 February. Once again Pepsi were signed up as major sponsors for the tour in what was claimed to be the largest sponsorship deal of all time. There was additional money earned from HBO too, for they would pay some $20 million for exclusive broadcast rights, proof that Michael could still earn major deals without John Branca. The tour would commence in June in Munich and much of the proceeds would be directed to his recently formed Heal The World foundation (named after one of the tracks on the *Dangerous* album), a foundation that would be devoted to helping underprivileged children around the world.

As lofty as Michael's plans were for all underprivileged children, it was to be a chance meeting with just one that would nearly bring Michael's world crashing down. Although Michael had learned to drive some years previously, he was not a particularly confident driver nor was he knowledgeable about cars themselves. When his jeep broke down on Wilshire Boulevard, therefore, his first instinct was to ring the emergency services on his mobile. Since his dilemma didn't qualify as an emergency, he stood by the side of the road wondering what he was going to do and who he was going to call next. Quite by chance he was not too far away from the offices of a car rental company and had been spotted by the disbelieving wife of an employee of the company. After a phone call to her husband, who told the rental company owner who in turn called his wife and asked her to bring her son (and his stepson) to the office, a veritable reception committee awaited Michael Jackson when he walked into the building.

The owner, Dave Schwartz, was the second husband of June Chandler-Schwartz. Her first marriage to dentist Evan Chandler had produced their own child protégé in Jordie Chandler, whose future talents appeared to be in the film world. He had come up with the idea for a parody of the hit Kevin Costner film *Robin Hood Prince Of Thieves* that he and his father, together with a family friend, had worked up into *Robin Hood Men In Tights* that was subsequently made into a major film. Jordie had been a fan of Michael's from an early age; when Michael had been burned filming the Pepsi commercial in 1984, the then four years old Jordie had written a letter expressing his hope that Michael would recover and received a pair of tickets to see Michael in concert for his trouble.

Dave Schwartz and the rest of the team at the car rental

company helped sort out Michael's predicament with his car and the initial meeting ended with June giving Michael the telephone number of her 12-year-old son. Michael would call Jordie a week later and then maintain telephone contact for the next nine months or so while out on the road with the Dangerous tour.

Meanwhile, the singles would continue to be pulled off the parent album as the months progressed; 'In The Closet' hit #6 US and #8 UK in April, 'Jam' would peak at #26 in the US in July and #12 in the UK in September, 'Who Is It' would become a UK Top Ten hit in July, with its release in the US delayed until February 1993, when it made #14. 'Heal The World' was a major European hit in December 1992, peaking at #2 in the UK (it was kept off the top spot by Whitney Houston's 'I Will Always Love You', which held residence for ten weeks) and selling more than half a million copies, 'Give In To Me' matched its predecessor's chart position in February 1993, 'Will You Be There', which was also featured in the film *Free Willy* hit #9 in July 1993 and the final UK single 'Gone Too Soon' made #33 in November. Overall the singles pulled from the album performed better than any previous Michael Jackson album; of the nine singles lifted from the album in the UK, seven made the Top Ten, with one topping the chart. In the US his chart performances were no less impressive, resulting in four Top Ten hits out of seven chart hits. The album had been quickly certified multi-platinum in the US, eventually selling some seven million copies in that territory alone. *Dangerous* would also be certified six times platinum in the UK (1.8 million copies) and six times platinum in Canada (600,000 units). It was in the emerging countries that Michael enjoyed his greatest growth in sales however, and *Dangerous* would go on to sell more than 32 million copies around the world, making this a bigger success than *Bad*. It might have gone on to become an even bigger seller too, for a video clip for 'Dangerous' was made by David Lynch for a proposed single release at the tail end of 1993, but by then Michael had other problems to confront.

The first leg of the world tour ended with eight sell-out concerts at the Tokyo Dome in Japan in December 1992, after which Michael returned home to Neverland. Television and promotional appearances kept him busy for the next two months or so, culminating in a stunning performance during the half time entertainment at the XXVII Superbowl between the Dallas Cowboys and Buffalo Bills at the Rose Bowl in Pasadena, a performance that was seen by some 133.4 million viewers. Less than two weeks later, he invited Oprah Winfrey to Neverland for her to conduct a candid interview, his first television interview for some 14 years.

Rather than the bland, staged interview many had expected, Michael was remarkably open about many aspects of his life. He admitted to 'crying through loneliness at age eight. I didn't have any friends growing up. I'd wash my face in the dark and my father would tease me. He was very strict.' He admitted to having been in love twice and was dating Brooke Shields but stated that he was a gentleman when pushed on whether or not he was still a virgin. On the question of the lightening of his skin colour, Michael revealed 'I have a skin disorder [Vitiligo] which destroys the pigment of my skin. It's in my family. We're trying to control it. I am a black American.' At the end of the interview, which had been conducted inside the house and while walking through his funfair, Michael introduced the world premier of the video clip to 'Give In

To Me'. The interview was seen by an audience of some 90 million viewers, another perfect piece of promotion by the King of Pop. During the interview Michael had also confirmed that this moniker was not self-imposed but had been given to him by friend Elizabeth Taylor during a presentation in 1989 – the name had stuck.

The day after the interview, Michael called Jordie and invited the youngster, his mother and his half-sister Lily to come and visit for the weekend. All of the amenities of Neverland were put at their disposal, culminating in a shopping trip to a toy store at which Michael spent tens of thousands of dollars on gifts for his new friends. The following weekend Michael journeyed down to June's home in Los Angeles to collect the three for a further stay at Neverland, but this time he had another young friend, Brett Barnes (who was introduced as Brett Jackson, a cousin) in tow, so Jordie did not have Michael's undivided attention during this second trip to the ranch.

Over the next few weeks the relationship between Michael Jackson and Jordie, June and to an extent Lily grew ever closer. For June it offered some respite from the fact that her marriage to Dave Schwartz was failing, as well as a brief glimpse of the life of luxury that Michael Jackson enjoyed. Not all of the get-togethers took place at Neverland, for Michael also maintained something of a hideaway in Los Angeles on Wilshire Boulevard, some ten minutes or so drive from the Schwartz's home. There were also first class trips to such locations as Las Vegas, with all four staying in Michael's suite at the Mirage Hotel.

It was the night after the Las Vegas trip that June became aware that her son might be sleeping with Michael. On getting up early one morning and going off in search of his son, she found his bed had not been slept in all night. As she searched the Neverland ranch, she came across Jordie in the process of sneaking out of Michael's room. While his explanation appeared innocent enough – Michael and Jordie had been watching *The Exorcist* in Michael's bedroom and Jordie had been too scared to leave after the film finished – the fact that the pair had shared a bed was of sufficient alarm for June to tell Jordie that such an event should not happen again.

As any concerned parent would have done, June felt compelled to raise the issue with Michael. His reaction was one of utter disappointment, since the implication appeared to be that there was something untoward occurring. Whatever Michael said had the desired affect, because June accepted the explanation that the friendship between Michael and Jordie was just that, a friendship. When June, Jordie and Lily made subsequent trips to either Neverland or the hideout, it was accepted that Jordie would share Michael's bedroom.

While June may have accepted the rather bizarre relationship between her son and Michael Jackson, her ex-husband Evan Chandler did not. As Jordie grew closer to Michael, it seemed to be at the expense of his relationship with his own father. It was bad enough that Michael was showering Jordie with expensive gifts that Evan could not afford, but when Michael was also buying gifts that were in Evan's price range, he became quite perturbed by the relationship.

In May 1993 Michael took June, Jordie and Lily with him on a trip to Monaco, where Michael was to collect a number of awards at the World Music Awards. As with all these type of awards in general, and with Michael in particular, there was a slew of paparazzi on hand to snap the foursome throughout their stay on the French Riviera. One of these pictures subsequently appeared in the

National Enquirer magazine with the caption 'Michael's New Adopted Family.' Evan saw the article and decided to confront Michael when they all returned from Europe. It was said that when Evan Chandler spoke to Michael, he asked him directly whether he was having sex with his son. Michael denied it (although according to several reports, perhaps not so vehemently as might be expected under the circumstances) and for a while Evan accepted that the relationship between the pair might well be as innocent as they both claimed.

Evan's doubts wouldn't fully subside, however, and although he welcomed Michael into his home at first, he eventually felt it would be better for all concerned if the pair kept a safe distance from each other. When he learned that Michael intended taking Jordie, June and Lily on the second leg of his world tour, he decided enough was enough and used a prior custody agreement to prevent his son from spending too much time with Michael. This action drove a wedge between Evan and June and also between Dave Schwartz and Evan. The two men would have a number of telephone arguments over the situation, with Dave Schwartz subsequently secretly taping one such conversation, during which he attempted to find out exactly what Evan hoped to achieve. It soon became apparent that Evan Chandler had already engaged a lawyer to handle a prospective case. 'There was no reason why he had to stop calling me... I picked the nastiest son of a bitch I could find [Larry Feldman], all he wants to do is get this out in the public as fast as he can, as big as he can and humiliate as many people as he can. He's nasty, he's mean, he's smart and he's hungry for publicity. Everything's going to a certain plan that isn't just mine. Once I make that phone call, this guy is going to destroy everybody in sight in any devious, nasty, cruel way that he can do it. I've given him full authority to do that. Jackson is an evil guy, he is worse than that and I have the evidence to prove it. If I go through with this, I win big-time. There's no way I lose. I will get everything I want and they will be destroyed forever... Michael's career will be over... It will be a massacre if I don't get what I want. It's going to be bigger than all us put together... This man is going to be humiliated beyond belief... He will not sell one more record.'

There was still one more part of Evan Chandler's armour that had to be secured; confirmation one way or another that the relationship between his son and Michael had developed into something more than just a friendship. When Jordie visited his father's dental practice for a routine tooth extraction, Evan Chandler used the opportunity to administer Sodium Amytal, supposedly used as something of a truth serum. While Jordie was at the very least groggy from the medicine and operation, Evan asked him specifically about his relationship with Michael and in particular whether there had been any sexual contact between them. Jordie confirmed that there had, although he didn't go into specific details and Evan didn't push him at the time.

According to later reports, Evan used his new found information to confront Michael and eventually submit a demand for some $20 million or the matter would be handed over to a criminal investigation. While Michael's initial reaction was that this was quite plainly an extortion attempt and that Evan Chandler could go to hell, his legal team made a number of counter offers, including a proposal for a number of film scripts that Michael would fund. This was turned down, and Evan reduced the sum of money he was seeking to $15 million, a deal that was also rejected. A further counter offer from Michael Jackson's team (which actually offered less in monetary terms than the original offer) was also turned down, at which point Evan Chandler decided it was time to carry through with his threat to turn the matter into a criminal investigation.

Before approaching the police, Evan arranged for his son to see a psychiatrist. During the three hour session, Jordie described in considerable detail exactly the sexual activity he said he and Michael had engaged in, which included kissing, masturbation and oral sex. These allegations were subsequently repeated to the police, as well as a detailed description of Michael's anatomy that would either prove or disprove what Jordie had said had transpired between him and Michael.

On 15 August Michael kicked off the second leg of his Dangerous World Tour, without Jordie, June or Lily being with him in Hong Kong. Three days later, the Los Angeles Police Department's Sexually Exploited Child Unit launched a criminal investigation into Michael's activities, with a search warrant obtained allowing them to search his Neverland ranch and his hideaway in downtown Los Angeles. A police officer involved in the case would subsequently tell the *Los Angeles Times* that no evidence to support the allegations had been found at either location, while June would also claim that she did not believe Michael had molested her son. However, Michael's team decided to go on the attack and on 24 August held a press conference at which they revealed that Evan Chandler had tried to extort $20 million in order for the allegations to go away. They omitted to mention that they had spent two months in negotiation or that they had made a number of counter proposals. The following day, two of Michael's other young friends, Brett Barnes and

Wade Robson, were drafted into another press conference to announce that they had slept in the same bed as Michael on several occasions and that nothing sexual had ever occurred. With hindsight, allowing two such young boys to make any statement, least of all one that confirmed that Michael was in the habit of sleeping with young boys, was not the best of strategies to employ.

As was to be expected, there were several others close to the singer who could be relied upon to state his case forcibly. The Jackson family came out and offered their total support for their son and brother, adding that as far as they were concerned this was almost certainly the action of a man trying to extract money from Michael Jackson. At much the same time, the police were conducting a behind-the-scenes investigation into Evan Chandler himself and had discovered that he was some $68,000 behind on child maintenance payments. This was despite holding a well paid job as a dentist and having been partly responsible for a moderate film success. At this point, the case appeared to be going against Evan Chandler.

Yet not everyone had such total faith in Michael's side of the story, with his sister LaToya being the first to break rank. As far as she was concerned, her brother was a paedophile and she had proof, although she would require payment of at least $500,000 to reveal her evidence. Intense negotiations were conducted with Jack Gordon (now her husband as well as her manager) and the tabloids on either side of the Atlantic, but these were ultimately doomed to failure, as it soon became apparent that LaToya had no evidence whatsoever. This did not silence her, however, for in Israel she felt compelled to state 'I cannot and will not be a silent collaborator in his crimes against young children. Forget about the superstar, forget about the icon. If he was any other 35-year-old man who was sleeping with little boys, you wouldn't like this guy.' She further backed this up by claiming that Michael had bought the silence of several other families in the past and that his actions were as a direct result of him having been abused as a child. Many, if not all, of her allegations eventually fell apart, with LaToya subsequently claiming that she had been put up to the story by her husband in order that they might gain financially from the predicament her brother found himself in.

There were many others who also saw the opportunity to make substantial sums of money from a story that was news all across the globe. Numerous past and present employees of Michael's at his Neverland ranch came forward with stories of alleged sexual misconduct. Unfortunately, all of these stories were directed towards the media; not one such story was submitted to the police and their ongoing investigation. Then again, the going rate for such stories had quickly topped the $100,000 (for claiming that Michael had sexually caressed Macaulay Culkin) and the $500,000 mark (for claiming that Michael had put his hand down Culkin's trousers). Both of these allegations were denied by Macaulay Culkin and his family. There was equally big money to be made where the alleged victim was unidentified. A former security guard claimed he was fired because he knew too much about what Michael was up to and had been ordered to destroy a photo of a naked boy, a story that was carried by one tabloid in return for payment of $150,000.

With his employees and even a member of his own family turning against him, Michael was in need of as many friends as he could get. Those who had been part of his inner circle for years, such as Elizabeth Taylor, Elton

John, Katherine Hepburn, Diana Ross and their ilk could all be relied upon for giving him their total and committed support. Yet to a man and woman, they all belonged to a different era. What Michael needed was a friend nearer his own age, someone he could confide in. He found it in perhaps the unlikeliest of places; Lisa Marie Presley.

Michael had first met Lisa Marie in 1974, when he was performing at the MGM Grand. As the only child of musical legend Elvis Presley, Lisa Marie had grown up in extravagant luxury, protected from much of the outside world by her father. Her father died unexpectedly in 1977, when she was eleven, and her world became even more confused than it had been while he was alive. Lisa Marie would eventually become something of a rebel, marrying her first husband in 1988 and having two children with him before they divorced. Michael and Lisa Marie were re-introduced by a mutual friend in 1993, and while Michael was on tour he found Lisa Marie to be someone he could rely upon for emotional support as the publicity around him became more and more negative. The pair spoke virtually every day, with Lisa Marie later stating 'I believed he didn't do anything wrong and that he was wrongly accused and yes, I started falling for him. I wanted to save him. I felt I could do it.'

Whatever the nature of the telephone calls when they began their relationship, as the months slipped by Michael came to rely on Lisa Marie more and more. Eventually during the autumn he enquired 'If I asked you to marry me, would you do it?' The answer would come several months later, but in the meantime Lisa Marie's support, together with that of his more reliable friends and associates, enabled Michael to keep up appearances, at least to a certain extent.

While the story got bigger and bigger and the allegations more lurid, Michael continued his world tour, although his health was beginning to falter both from the physical exertions of the tour and the mental stress he was undoubtedly under. Several dates were cancelled and, apparently, Michael became even more reliant on drugs and painkillers, including Valium, Xanax and Ativan, with the end result he lost more weight and stopped eating. It became a vicious circle and ultimately Michael decided to call a halt to the tour. His first port of call was to London with Elizabeth Taylor and a planned stay with Elton John's then manager John Reid, but after virtually collapsing when he arrived at the airport, he was admitted to a clinic where he underwent group and one-to-one therapy.

Eventually Michael decided that his best course of action was to return home and face the music. He arrived home on 10 December 1993, with a search warrant being presented soon after his arrival that allowed the investigators to conduct a strip search in order to verify the description Jordie Chandler had given of Michael's anatomy. The District Attorney (Tom Sneddon), a detective, photographer and doctor were therefore able to 'examine, photograph and videotape' his entire body, 'including his penis, anus, hips, buttocks and any other part of his body.' Any refusal to comply on Michael's part would be used in court as a possible indication of guilt. The 25 minute ordeal was conducted inside Michael's Neverland ranch, with Michael subsequently appearing on satellite television to state 'As you may already know, after my tour ended I remained out of the country undergoing treatment for a dependency on pain medication... There have been many disgusting statements made recently concerning allegations of improper conduct

on my part. These statements about me are totally false...
I will say I am particularly upset by the handling of the
matter by the incredible, terrible mass media. At every
opportunity, the media has dissected and manipulated
these allegations to reach their own conclusions. I ask
all of you to wait and hear the truth before you label or
condemn me. Don't treat me like a criminal, because I am
innocent. I have been forced to submit to a dehumanizing
and humiliating examination... It was the most humiliating
ordeal of my life... But if this is what I have to endure to
prove my innocence, my complete innocence, so be it.'

As serious as the allegations undoubtedly were, there
were many who believed that Michael was entirely
innocent. As far as many polls were concerned, where
sometimes as many as 80% of those polled expressed
support for Michael, the singer was being tried and
effectively convicted by the media, aided by leaks from
inside the police investigation.

In addition to the criminal case being prepared by
the Los Angeles Police Department, Evan Chandler had
instructed his lawyer to commence a civil suit against
Michael. On 11 January 1994 (incidentally Jordie's 14th
birthday) Chandler's lawyer filed a number of papers
with the Los Angeles Superior Court, including testimony
from a number of ex-employees of Michael's, all of
whom would be confirming the allegations made against
their former employer. Most damaging of all, however,
was a request from the Chandler team to be allowed
access to Michael Jackson's financial records. At this
point, Michael listened to the advice of his legal team
and friends, searched his own heart and mind and opted
to settle. Although both parties signed a legal agreement
confirming strict confidentiality as to the settlement terms,

it subsequently became almost common knowledge that Michael Jackson paid a total of $22 million to Jordie, his mother June and the prosecution attorney Larry Feldman, payable over a period of years. The close relationship that had sprung up between Michael and Jordie evaporated in an instant – the pair never spoke to each other again. June's marriage to Dave Schwartz subsequently collapsed, while her first husband Evan tried to sue Michael for a further $60 million in 1996, claiming Michael had breached the confidentiality agreement – the case was thrown out of court in 1999.

The settlement of the civil suit saw the collapse of the criminal charges too, for Jordie would not testify in a criminal trial. Without a witness, star or otherwise, the police and grand jury decided that they could not press charges with the existing evidence and Michael Jackson was not charged with any crime. The stain on his character, however, was considerable.

When it was all finally over, Michael was asked why he had paid off his accuser. 'I wanted to go on with my life. Too many people had already been hurt. I want to make records. I want to sing. I want to perform again... It's my talent. My hard work. My life. My decision.'

Some decisions, of course, were taken out of Michael's hands. The Dangerous tour was halted early, the release of the *Dangerous* single was cancelled, the launch of a fragrance was halted and planned involvement in the film *Addams Family Values*, for which Michael had written and recorded a number of specific songs, was dropped. Most tellingly, a ten-year partnership between Michael and Pepsi was also ended, even though having Michael Jackson on board had grossed the company some $500 million during the decade. When Michael's more ardent fans found out that he had been unceremoniously dumped by the soft drinks company they organised a boycott of Pepsi products. The share value dropped by *20%* the following year!

CHAPTER TWELVE
SHE DRIVES ME WILD

There is little doubt that Michael's reputation took a severe battering once news of the settlement was released. Even those who had previously backed him unhesitatingly began to have their doubts. Was he innocent or guilty? And how could his career, that which was most dear to him, ever recover from such a low? There was one friend who remained loyal throughout the entire period, who gave him wise counsel when he needed it and had frequently advised him to settle, irrespective of guilt or otherwise, in order that he could move his life on the next stage: Lisa Marie Presley.

While much of their early relationship had been conducted via telephone during Michael's tour, the pair became inseparable when Michael returned to the United States. And it wasn't just two friends spending as much time as they possibly could with each other. Close friends sensed that a deeper relationship was growing. Michael had perhaps been the first to recognise a kindred spirit in Lisa Marie, which had been one of the reasons he had suggested marriage a few months previously. Now, Lisa Marie was beginning to warm to the idea, even though she was still technically married to her first husband Danny Keough at the time (Lisa Marie would fly to the Dominican Republic early in May 1994 to arrange a quick divorce, although she and Danny remain good friends to this day). The couple shared idyllic moments together at Michael's Neverland ranch and a few days away together in Florida, with numerous reports of the couple walking hand in hand and kissing and cuddling beginning to emerge.

As far as the cynical were concerned, this sudden heterosexual relationship on Michael's part was little more than a publicity stunt on par with his earlier escapades. How convenient, they would claim, that a man who had only recently been embroiled in a paedophile investigation should suddenly be dating such a glamorous woman. Of course, there were countless precedents for such behaviour. The likes of Rock Hudson, Tab Hunter and Raymond Burr had either married or had relationships of convenience in order to stave off ongoing rumours about their sexuality.

Irrespective of Michael's reputation at the time, there would still have been countless women interested in dating the King of Pop, yet many of these would have been attracted by the wealth and fame rather than the man underneath it all. Michael already had countless hangers-on. The last thing he needed was one with a romantic interest in him.

Yet Lisa Marie Presley was no Phyllis Gates, Debbie Reynolds or Natalie Wood. As the heir to Elvis Presley, she was (and is) independently wealthy and, as she had proven time and again, very much her own woman. There is no way Lisa Marie would have allowed herself to be used as a pawn in a publicity campaign for Michael, best friend or not. As Lisa Marie would later state 'Our relationship was not a "sham". It was an unusual relationship, where two unusual people who did not live, or know, a "normal life" found a connection, perhaps with some suspect timing on his part. Nonetheless, I do believe he loved me as much as he could love anyone. I wanted to "save him" from the inevitable. His family and his loved ones also wanted to save him from this as well but didn't know how. But in trying to save him, I almost lost myself.'

Cynicism apart, the eventual marriage between Michael

Jackson and Lisa Marie Presley made perfect sense, for who else would the King of Pop choose as his bride than the woman who would become the Princess of Rock & Roll, the only daughter of the King of Rock & Roll. The marriage between the pair was as close to a royal wedding as the American music industry was ever likely to see!

Less than three weeks after her divorce from Danny Keough was finalised, Lisa Marie and Michael were married in La Vega in the Dominican Republic, by civil judge Hugh Francisco Alverez Perez. To say it was a low key affair would be an understatement. Neither told their family or friends and even denied they had been married for fully two months after the event. And if either had ever previously dreamed of having a ceremony to remember the day they got married, they were both underwhelmed by the event. Michael would later claim that it was because they both feared a massive media intrusion that they had opted for privacy, but of course countless celebrities had married before and since and managed to control the media coverage.

There was to be no honeymoon either, for Michael was about to start recording his next album, which would eventually emerge in June 1995 as *HIStory: Past, Present And Future Book 1*. Michael had decided that John Branca's earlier suggestion for a career retrospective made sound business sense now that he had been at the top of the musical tree for the best part of 15 years. Thus the first disc of the planned two-disc package was to feature 15 of his biggest hits culled from *Off The Wall, Thriller, Bad* and *Dangerous*. The second disc would contain a total of fifteen new songs, and Michael had plenty of inspiration for those!

The primary focus for the new songs was the media,

which Michael blamed for virtually all of the ills that had plagued him over the previous few years. District Attorney Tom Sneddon did not escape either, being the subject of the song 'D.S.' (in the chorus Michael changes the name of the subject to Dom Sheldon, possibly in order to avoid a potential lawsuit. Sneddon later commented 'I have not, shall we say, done him the honour of listening to it, but I've been told that it ends with the sound of a gunshot').

Michael had also moved on from Teddy Riley, utilising the assistance of James Harris and Terry Lewis, better known as Jam & Lewis, on a number of tracks. Jam & Lewis had scored major success with another member of the Jackson clan, Janet, including two albums in *Control* and *Rhythm Nation 1814* that had actually given Michael's success a run for its money. When Michael asked Janet to contribute to the song 'Scream', she eagerly accepted. Indeed, in her words she felt she 'had made it to the top' and had no need to fear that she 'had to ride Michael's coattails'. Other contributors included Robert Kelly (better known as R Kelly, who would have his own legal battles concerning underage sexual activity in the future), Dallas Austin and David Foster. Assisting on vocal duties were Motown vocal group Boyz II Men and rappers The Notorious B.I.G. and Shaquille O'Neal. Also included on the album were two cover versions, 'Come Together', a Beatles song credited to John Lennon and Paul McCartney (for which Michael owned the publishing!) and 'Smile', written by Charles Chaplin and originally a hit for Nat King Cole in 1954, although it enjoyed a new lease of life in 1993 when Robert Downey performed it in the film biography *Chaplin*. Michael would claim it was his favourite song of all time.

In many aspects of his life and career, the recording

of *HIStory* was very much business as usual for Michael Jackson. There was a promotional campaign to put together, another world tour to organise and videos to shoot. 'You Are Not Alone' featured a near nude Michael and Lisa Marie and attracted considerable controversy. Similarly, 'They Don't Care About Us' showed Michael singing the song in a prison and was subsequently dropped from the MTV playlist because of the scenes of violence throughout. This version was in fact the second version of the video that had been shot, as Michael and director Spike Lee had earlier filmed a version that was shot in a shanty town in Brazil. That version was pulled after Michael attracted some criticism from a local politician who thought Michael was exploiting poverty.

As the videos and songs began to come together, Michael appeared at a Sony Music product presentation in January 1995 to announce the release of *HIStory* during the coming summer. Sony of Japan had paid $2 billion for CBS Records in November 1987 and had formed Sony Music Entertainment in 1991 out of the company. The release would be accompanied by a world tour and there were going to be some extra special promotional plans to accompany the release.

The whole campaign commenced with the release of the double A side single 'Scream' and 'Childhood', the former featuring Michael's sister Janet. The single would register the then highest ever entry onto the Billboard Hot 100 when it opened at #5. In the UK it entered at #3, yet on both sides of the Atlantic it stalled at its opening positions, despite a subsequent remix (which entered the UK chart in its own right) and the most expensive accompanying video ever produced which cost $7 million. There would be some payback however, for 'Scream' would win the

Grammy Award for Best Music Video Short Form.

A week before the album was released, the promotional campaign that had been devised began to reach fever pitch. The cover to the album featured a statue-like image of Michael dressed in usual military influenced tunic. A 10-metre high model weighing some 2,100 kilos was loaded onto a barge on the River Thames and sailed under Tower Bridge. The stunt was repeated in numerous capitals around Europe and obviously worked: *HIStory* debuted on the UK charts at number one and would go on to sell over 1.2 million copies, an extremely impressive figure for what was an expensive double album.

Indeed, if *HIStory* had been a single album, its sales figures would have been close to rivalling *Thriller*, for the album would sell over 20 million copies worldwide and is the bestselling double-disc album of all time. In the US the album entered the chart at number one and spent two weeks at the summit on its way to being certified platinum seven times over. In all, the album sold more than six million copies in Europe, including more than a million copies each in France, Germany and the UK. Michael's European fans had always been among his most loyal and proved it beyond doubt with their acceptance of *HIStory*.

The album's second single 'You Are Not Alone' also entered the Billboard charts at its peak. On 2 September 1995 it became the first single ever to enter the Billboard Hot 100 at number one, beating the previous record held by 'Scream'. Written by R Kelly, the single was a success around the world, topping the UK charts and selling a total of three million copies, including one million in the US. Later two Belgian songwriters, brothers Eddy and Danny Van Passel, would claim to have written the melody as 'If We Can Start All Over' in 1993 and launched a plagiarism suit against R Kelly. In September 2007 a judge ruled in favour of the Van Passel's and 'You Are Not Alone' was subsequently banned from the airwaves of Belgian radio.

A further three singles were lifted from *HIStory* in Europe: 'Earth Song', which topped the UK charts for six weeks and sold over a million copies, making it his most successful single in that territory (it would sell some 3.15 million copies worldwide), 'They Don't Care About Us', which was a #4 UK and #30 US hit, and 'Stranger In Moscow', which matched its predecessor's chart position in the UK. Michael also linked up with Tai, Tarryll and TJ Jackson, the sons of Tito and therefore Michael's nephews on, 'Why', a #2 UK hit in August 1996.

By the time the last of the singles had been lifted from the album, there had once again been major upheaval in Michael's life. While he and Lisa Marie may have presented to the world a picture of idyllic married life, the reality behind the scenes was anything but. It has been suggested that Lisa Marie entered into marriage with Michael in order that he might help her attain her ambition of securing a recording contract (she would eventually land a contract with Capitol in 2000, although her debut album finally appeared three years later). While he certainly offered to assist and encourage her career, Michael had other career priorities during the 18 months or so the pair were together, not least rescuing his own blighted reputation. There is little doubt as to what exactly Michael wanted from Lisa Marie – children. The sleeve notes to *HIStory* had given an indication of the depth of feeling Michael held for children. 'To honour the children of the world, I vow to keep my promise to help the sick and dying, the alone, homeless and hungry, through the construction of children's hospitals and orphanages in every needy corner of the world'. Yet what he wanted more than anything was children of his own. By all accounts and for whatever reason, Lisa Marie refused.

There were other cracks appearing in their relationship even as they were telling the world how much they were in love. A televised interview with the pair and Diane Sawyer on ABC's *Primetime Live* in June 1995 was a public relations disaster, at least for Michael. Watched by some 60 million viewers, Michael gave a childish performance, not appreciating the concern in several of the questions relating to the recently settled civil suit. When asked if he was likely to have young friends stay for sleepovers in the future, Michael said he undoubtedly would, since as far as he was concerned, everything he had engaged in previously was entirely innocent. Attempts by Lisa Marie to explain such behaviour as 'normal' as far as Michael Jackson was concerned served only to drop him deeper into the mire. Yet even as Lisa Marie was trying to assist, Michael couldn't resist belittling the seriousness of the occasion by making hand signals behind his wife's head.

When Michael was booked to appear on the MTV Video Music Awards, he arranged for Lisa Marie to join him on stage. Before the pair walked hand in hand to the podium, Lisa Marie sternly told Michael that on no account should they kiss on stage, that it was tacky. Michael ignored the advice and duly gave her a steamy embrace that only served to add to the rumours that everything about Michael and Lisa Marie was a publicity stunt, including their marriage.

In January 1996, Lisa Marie filed for divorce citing 'irreconcilable differences'. There had been no pre-nuptial agreement between the pair, and no details of any financial settlement were published after the divorce. Yet the 18-month marriage had raised other issues for Lisa Marie. 'I became very ill and emotionally and spiritually exhausted in my quest to save him from certain self-destructive behaviour and from the awful vampires and leeches he would always manage to magnetise around him. I was in over my head while trying. I had my children to care for. I had to make a decision, which was to walk away and let his fate have him, even though I desperately loved him and tried to stop or reverse it somehow.'

'After the divorce I spent a few years obsessing about him and what I could have done different. Then I spent some angry years with whole situation and then at some point, I truly became indifferent.'

Writing in the immediate aftermath of Michael's death, Lisa Marie went on to give further insights to the demons that were troubling Michael during their marriage. 'As I sit here overwhelmed with sadness and confusion at what was [my] biggest failure to date, watching the news almost play the exact scenario I saw happen on 16 August 1977 [the death of her father Elvis] happening again, right now with Michael just as he predicted. Michael and I were having a deep conversation about life in general. At some point he stared at me very intensely and he stated with an almost calm certainty 'I'm afraid that I am going to end up like him, the way he did' [referring to Elvis Presley]. I tried to deter him from the idea, at which point he just shrugged his shoulders and nodded as if to let me know, he knew what he knew, and that was that. A predicted ending by him, by loved ones, and by me – but what I didn't predict was how much it was going to hurt when it finally happened. I am truly, truly, gutted. Any ill experience or words I have felt towards him in the past has just died inside of me, along with him.'

Lisa Marie would go on to marry actor Nicholas Cage

in 2002 and divorce him two years later. In 2006 she married for a third time, to musician Michael Lockwood.

At the same time that Michael's marriage with Lisa Marie was unravelling, another merger was occupying his mind. In November 1995 Sony announced that after intense negotiations, they had entered into an agreement with Michael to merge his Northern Songs catalogue with theirs to form Sony/ATV Music Publishing. Under the deal, Michael would receive an upfront payment of $95 million from Sony, even though the deal did not include the rights to any of his own compositions, which would remain with Warner Chappell.

The money-making machine that was Michael Jackson still showed no sign of slowing up. The HIStory tour had become one of the biggest tours in the world, performing a total of 82 concerts in 58 cities and attracting over 4.5 million fans, making it the most successful tour of his career. There had been controversial moments, not all of which were of Michael's making. In February 1996 he accepted an invitation to perform at the annual BRIT Awards at Earl's Court, where he was also to receive the Artist of a Generation Award, with Michael opting to perform 'Earth Song' (the single had just vacated the Top Ten after nine weeks, including six weeks on top of the charts). Michael had hired a number of children to join him, but the performance was interrupted midway through the song when Pulp frontman Jarvis Cocker wandered onto the stage and wiggled his backside towards the audience. As security struggled to remove Cocker from the stage, a number of the performing children were injured. Cocker was later arrested (but not charged) and defended his actions by stating it was 'a form of protest at the way Michael Jackson sees himself as some Christ-like figure with the power of healing.'

By the time the HIStory tour came to an end, Michael had remarried. When Michael's skin problem had first been diagnosed as vitiligo in the mid 1980s, he had visited a dermatologist, where a young nurse named Debbie Rowe was an assistant. Over the course of the next ten years or so, Michael and Debbie developed something of a friendship, with Debbie being on hand to offer the same kind of emotional support that likes of Elizabeth Taylor and Lisa Marie were also providing. According to reports, the relationship was another that grew over the years, with Debbie appearing to be something of a devoted fan (her apartment was said to have numerous pictures and posters of Michael, all of which had been signed over the years). There were also suggestions that the relationship between Debbie and Michael continued even after Michael had married Lisa Marie and that Lisa Marie was aware of it, even though she did not believe that Debbie Rowe presented a real threat to her marriage.

Yet the evidence would suggest that Debbie Rowe was a real threat for one reason – she was more than prepared to give Michael the child he so desperately craved. Indeed, it has been said that as his marriage crumbled over the fact that Lisa Marie did not want to have any more children, Michael told her that he had found someone (Debbie) who was prepared to get pregnant for him. Lisa Marie's reaction was said to be a somewhat dismissive 'go ahead.'

Even as the divorce papers were being drawn up, Michael had taken Lisa Marie at her word. Debbie Rowe was pregnant. Indeed, by the time the divorce was finalised, Debbie was five months into her pregnancy term, having been artificially inseminated. As with everything connected with Michael Jackson, the news of the pregnancy was splashed on the front cover of a magazine after Debbie had a private conversation with a 'friend' that was tape-recorded and duly sold to *The News of the World.* The article also stated that Debbie would be paid some $500,000 for delivering the baby to Michael.

Michael went on the defensive to claim that Debbie had not been artificially inseminated and that there had been no economic relationship between them, but neither statement was strongly believed. Unfortunately, Debbie suffered a miscarriage but in May 1996 was pregnant again, under the same circumstances and conditions. She believed that this time the pregnancy would go the full term.

Neither Michael nor Debbie saw any reason to marry simply because they were having a baby together. Michael had only recently ended his marriage to Lisa Marie and Debbie herself had previously been married, so neither was in any particular rush to get up the aisle. It was Katherine Jackson who would ultimately persuade them, since the idea of any baby being born out of wedlock was against her religious beliefs – something she had already experienced with her own husband. Therefore, on 14 November 1996, in Sydney, Australia – during the HIStory tour – Michael Joseph Jackson and Deborah Jeanne Rowe became man and wife, with Debbie now six months pregnant with the couple's child.

This time around there were considerably more people to witness the marriage. A total of 15 friends gathered at the Sheraton on the Park, with a young friend of Michael's called Anthony (aged just eight) the best man! But certain similarities existed between Michael's first and second marriage. There was no honeymoon and Debbie returned to the United States less than a week later, having not spent a single night with her new husband.

On 13 February 1997, at Cedars-Sinai Medical Center, Prince Michael Jackson was born. Michael was present at the birth and helped his wife cut the umbilical cord. Michael spent some five hours at the hospital before taking the new baby home with him to Neverland. He would later release a statement that said 'I have been blessed beyond comprehension and I will work tirelessly at being the best father I can be. I appreciate that my fans are elated, but I hope that everyone respects the privacy that Debbie and I want and need for our son. I grew up in a fish bowl and I will not allow that to happen to my son. Please give my son his privacy.'

Yet only a month later Michael, Debbie and Prince Michael were presented to the world at a press conference at the Four Seasons Hotel. To counter rumours that this was another marriage of convenience for Michael and that he had forbidden Debbie to see their son, he said 'That's completely false. We have been together as a family since the birth of our son, and we've cherished every moment as a family.'

The statement did not quell rumours that this was an economic relationship. It soon became known that there was a pre-nuptial agreement between the pair and stories swept the media that Debbie was paid $750,000 for the birth of their son and would receive a further $170,000 for every year they remained married. When Michael subsequently took his son off to Paris and Debbie remained domiciled in her modest Los Angeles apartment, it became apparent that while many things in Michael's life were not 'normal', a married couple on separate continents with the child being with the father was abnormal, to say the least.

It was to be Michael and his team of nannies that were

going to be responsible for bringing up the new child, with Debbie's input being minimal. Indeed, it was alleged that when Michael took the baby on the final stages of the HIStory tour, Debbie had only seen her four-month-old son twice! She would eventually link up with Michael during the French leg of the ongoing HIStory tour, where, according to later reports, she fell pregnant a third time. Another regular visitor during the last legs of the tour was Lisa Marie, who was as eager as Michael to ensure that their platonic relationship did not suffer as a result of the failure of their marriage. By all accounts the pair patched up their differences, with both claiming to have been in love with the other during their 18 months together. Unfortunately, Debbie Rowe's readiness and ability to give Michael what he most desired where Lisa Marie had not had eventually brought to an end their marriage.

In between juggling relationships with his former and current wives, Michael also found time for another album release, *Blood On The Dance Floor: HIStory In The Mix*, an album that remixed eight of the songs from the earlier *HIStory* release with five new songs in 'Blood On The Dance Floor', 'Morphine', 'Superfly Sister', 'Ghosts' and 'Is It Scary'. 'Blood On The Dance Floor' would become Michael's seventh and final UK number one, entering at pole position and spending nine weeks on the chart. A second single, which combined *History* with *Ghosts,* was released in July 1997 and peaked at #5. The album, however, would go on to sell some six million copies around the world, making it the most successful remix album of all time. It also topped the UK charts for two weeks, as opposed to the relatively lowly position of #24 it attained in the US.

On 3 April 1998 Debbie gave birth to the couple's

second child. A daughter that was named Paris-Michael Katherine (the Paris in her name was supposedly where the baby had been conceived), the upbringing arrangements were to be exactly as they were for Prince Michael. That the couple still did not enjoy a conventional marriage was not in doubt: to celebrate the safe delivery of the second child, Michael's gift to Debbie was a new house in Los Angeles! Soon after the baby's birth, Michael's representatives contacted the Vatican to see if the Pope would conduct the baby's christening. They were swiftly turned down, with the eventual note that was passed back stressing that the Pope had no wish to participate in what the Vatican saw as little more than a publicity stunt!

The Pope was probably nearer to the mark than even he realised, for having delivered two children to Michael, Debbie felt there was no longer any reason for them to remain man and wife. She asked for a divorce and was duly granted one in October 1999, the pre-nuptial agreement ensuring that she received no more than some $10 million and a house as her part of the settlement. In 2001 she applied to a judge to have her parental rights to Prince Michael and Paris-Michael terminated, thus leaving the upbringing entirely to the devices of Michael and whichever nannies and tutors he saw fit. For the most part, Debbie then settled into a relatively anonymous lifestyle and was occasionally mentioned in the media, but subsequent events in Michael's life meant that she was seldom far away. Indeed, her initial loyalty during some of his forthcoming darkest days was that of the most loyal of former employees. How Michael must have wished he had vetted his other members of staff as thoroughly as the woman who bore his children.

CHAPTER THIRTEEN

INVINCIBLE?

B y the turn of the century, Michael must have felt he was on top of the world. He had had the biggest selling album of all in time in *Thriller* and had released four others that were massive sellers, even if not at the same level as his original blockbuster. He was confirmed as the bestselling artist of all time by Guinness World Records, with estimates of 750 million units. He had earned a further entry in that august publication for his support of 39 charities, more than any other personality.

Under the guidance of John Branca, Michael's publishing interests had expanded almost tenfold. The $47 million that Michael had paid for the Northern Songs catalogue in 1985 was now worth an estimated $400 million, and was continuing to grow in both value and the number of copyrights. He had two children, something he had always craved, even if the relationships with both his wives had ended in divorce. Yet Michael had never believed he had to be married to be content, especially having observed at first hand how his parents were married in name only and that virtually all of his siblings had ended their marriages for one reason or another.

Besides, Michael had already begun work on his next album, his first proper studio recording in some six years. *Invincible* would find him working with Rodney Jerkins, Dr Freeze, Teddy Riley, Andre Harris, Babyface and R Kelly, who co-produced with Michael the 16 tracks on the album. Yet in spreading the production net so wide, *Invincible* emerged as an album without a central focus. The general consensus was that it was ultimately too long, running to almost 80 minutes in total. There were several strong potential singles on display and, as he had done countless times before, Michael gave consideration to video clips and promotional support for what was seen as an eagerly awaited comeback album.

Shortly before the planned release, however, Michael told Sony that the album would be his last for the label! As far as he was concerned, the licenses on his original material were soon to expire and the rights would revert back to him. He could either re-sign with Sony or he could shop around for an even more lucrative deal. There were plenty of companies who would be willing to do the kind of deal the likes of which the record industry hadn't seen before, with David Geffen likely to be at the head of the queue for his signature.

Yet the finer detail of the contract showed Michael was considerably out on his assumption as far as the reversion clause was concerned. There were still a considerable number of years still to run. When Michael realised that the rights would not revert when he expected them to, he launched an investigation and discovered that the attorney who had represented him had also represented Sony, thus creating a conflict of interest. It got more interesting the deeper Michael dug, for he soon spotted another potential conflict of interest that duly alarmed him. Sony had been pushing to buy out his share of their joint publishing company for several years, but while Michael remained independently wealthy he had no need to sell. However, if his financial situation should change and he needed to raise money quickly, his 50% share of Sony/ATV was undoubtedly the most valuable part of his portfolio. While his records were still selling in huge quantities (even if considerably lower than they had some 15 years previously) he was not financially troubled, but if his records didn't sell well and his income dropped significantly, the situation would change. As far as Michael was concerned, Sony now had a vested interest in wrecking his career and his income.

While Michael had always got on well with the old hands at Sony such as Walter Yetnikoff, he did not see eye-to-eye with the newer executives in charge, most notably Tommy Mottola. The phenomenal success of *Thriller* had given Michael extraordinary leverage at the company and, over the years, he had seen off many of the pretenders to his throne, including the likes of New Kids On The Block. While Michael's sales remained high, so did his status with the company, but now he was under pressure like never before. Mariah Carey had become a worldwide star (no doubt assisted by her one-time status as Mrs Mottola) as would Jennifer Lopez, Shakira and a host of others. Michael's subsequent announcement that he intended leaving the label should with hindsight have been made *after* the album was released. The result was that all video shoots and promotional campaigns were subsequently cancelled, leaving *Invincible* to sink or swim on its own merits.

The album did give rise to three singles, with 'You Rock My World' becoming a #10 hit in the US and peaking at #2 in the UK, where it was unable to topple Kylie Minogue's 'Can't Get You Out Of My Head' from the top spot. 'Cry' barely made the Top 30, peaking at #25 in the UK, while 'Butterflies' made it to #14 in the US. The lack of a video worked against 'Butterflies' in particular, and from being an eagerly anticipated release, *Invincible* became perceived as something of a disappointment as sales struggled to reach the ten million mark worldwide.

Michael was in no doubt as to where the blame lay, going public with his dispute with Tommy Mottola and accusing the executive of racism and Sony of deliberately not promoting the album. The label refuted all allegations, stating that Michael's refusal to tour the US had made promotion of the album difficult. They may well have had a point too, for even amid the allegations the album did top the charts on both sides of the Atlantic for a week and also headed the charts in 12 other countries. Indeed, its chart performance in the US was especially impressive given that it was up against Enrique Iglesias and a greatest hits package from the Backstreet Boys that same October 2001 week.

While Michael retired to licks his wounds after the relative failure of his latest album, there was another red letter event on the horizon: the birth of a third child in February 2002. This time Michael did not state who the mother was, claiming that this baby, to be named Prince Michael Jackson II, was the result of artificial insemination and a surrogate mother (Michael would also claim that his first two children had been the result of natural conception). At first Michael claimed not to know who the actual mother was, although he would later state that he had made sure that the mother was of good health and of good intellect. Further contradictions occurred when Michael stated that the mother was a black woman and later retracted this statement. Prince Michael Jackson II was, like his two siblings, almost certainly born to a white woman, with something closer to the real truth about the parentage of all three children only coming to light in the immediate aftermath of Michael's death.

Michael may have now been a father three times over but there were still moments when he appeared to have little clue as to how to behave like one, most notably when dangling the youngest child over the balcony of a hotel in Berlin after fans had screamed for a view. The resulting negative publicity saw Michael on the defensive, claiming that the baby had always been in his control and he would never harm any child, least of all one of his own. It was a statement Michael would have to repeat often in the coming months.

Ever since his exclusive interview with Oprah Winfrey in 1993, television companies the world over had been trying to get the same kind of access to Michael. Now, with his personal stock still recovering from two failed marriages and the Jordie Chandler case still relatively fresh in the memory, those requests became louder. There were two journalists/presenters in particular pushing for exclusive interviews, Louis Theroux and Martin Bashir.

Since direct access to Michael was impossible, anyone with proposals for him to consider would approach him through friends. Michael had become particularly friendly with psychic Uri Geller and had frequently visited him in England, accompanying him on trips to Harrods (where owner Mohamed Al Fayed was a mutual friend), the Houses of Parliament (where Michael had ignored protocol and sat in the House of Commons, even though the seating is only available to elected politicians), and Exeter City football club, where Geller was at one time on the board and serving as Uri's best man when he renewed his vows with his wife. Since Uri appeared to have Michael's ear, Martin Bashir in particular tried to convince him to persuade Michael to grant him an interview.

Bashir's reputation was certainly high, for he had previously interviewed Princess Diana, a woman Michael was known to greatly admire, and presented her in a sympathetic manner following the break up of her marriage to Prince Charles. Both Michael and Uri therefore felt that a detailed series of interviews, conducted between May 2002 and January 2003, would be something of a coup for both interviewer and interviewee.

It would be fair to say that Bashir was allowed access that no journalist before or since has ever had. He accompanied Michael on trips to Europe (and thus recorded the baby-over-the-balcony incident in Berlin), went on shopping sprees where Michael spent over a million dollars on furniture for a new house, and talked with him about the songwriting process. Michael showed Martin his dance moves, discussed his changing appearance, and touched upon how Debbie Rowe had effectively made a gift of his first two children, although he also contradicted himself when discussing the mother of Prince Michael Jackson II (who is also known by the name Blanket, an affectionate term that originated from Michael's own childhood.)

The controversy over the eventual programme *Living With Michael Jackson,* however, centred around the revelation that Michael still had young friends to stay for sleepovers and still allowed them to share his own bed. This time the youngster in question was Gavin Arvizo, a youngster born in 1989 who had been diagnosed with cancer in 2000, which had resulted in him having his spleen and a kidney removed. It was revealed that Gavin's medical expenses had been paid for by Michael and that Gavin and his family were regular and frequent visitors to Neverland. The footage showed Michael and Gavin holding hands and invariably Gavin would rest his head on Michael's shoulders.

The completed programme was duly aired on British

television on 3 February 2003 and in the US three days later. With Bashir's commentary working up the story about Michael's relationship with a number of young boys, it was no surprise that media and public reaction to the documentary should be so negative. In response, Michael produced his own programme (*Take Two: The Footage You Were Never Meant To See*) that featured interviews with assorted friends and colleagues, all of whom were defensive of Michael's actions.

It was not only the public and media who had watched the two documentaries with interest, for various officials within the Los Angeles Department of Family and Services, Santa Barbara Child Protective Services and the Los Angeles Child Welfare Department had also been alarmed enough to instigate independent investigations a week after the original Bashir programme aired. A further week later, both the DCFS and Los Angeles Police probes concluded that there was no foundation to allegations of abuse and brought their investigations to a halt. In April, the Santa Barbara County Department reached much the same conclusion and ended their investigation. That, seemingly, was the end of the matter.

In June, the matter was brought to the attention of the Santa Barbara County Sheriff's Department, as a result of a complaint made by the Arvizo family. The eventual charges and the background story revealed many similarities between the family of Gavin Arvizo and Michael's earlier accuser Jordie Chandler. Gavin's mother, Janet Ventura-Arvizo, was divorced from the boy's father and had initially seen Michael as something of a substitute father for her children, who in addition to the ill Gavin also included brother Star and sister Daveline. Initially, the whole Arvizo family had been supportive of

Michael, stating to all investigators that nothing untoward had occurred between Michael and any of the children. By June, however, the family had changed their story, claiming that molestation had occurred and had started on 7 February 2003, the day after the Martin Bashir documentary had originally aired in the United States.

There were certain elements of the Arvizo complaints that did warrant further investigation. According to the three children, Michael had plied them with alcohol during a flight from Florida in February. Although not a heavy drinker, Michael did enjoy the occasional glass of wine, but in order that his image not be tarnished, both red wine (or Jesus Blood, as Michael referred to it) and white wine (Jesus Juice) were served in Coke cans. While this simple ruse was well-known among Michael's inner circle, the fact that three children, the very people Michael was attempting to hoodwink with his subterfuge, were aware of it was certainly alarming.

However, as with the Jordie Chandler case, there were other elements of the story and the background of the family that did not add up, after even simple investigation. In 1998, for example, the family had been arrested on alleged shoplifting charges in a JC Penney store. According to the store, the boys had been sent out of the store with their arms laden with clothing and been detained, at which point Janet Arvizo had become involved in a scuffle with three security officers. The shoplifting charges were eventually dropped, but Janet Arvizo launched a $3 million suit against the store, claiming that she and her son Gavin had been beaten by the officers. Some two years later, with the case still not having reached the court, Janet added a further charge that she had been sexually molested by one of the security officers for some seven minutes. No mention of the abuse had been made in the original complaint, yet two years later Janet and her sons appeared to have perfect recollection of the events of that day. A few days before the case was due to be heard, JC Penney reached agreement with the Arvizo family and paid them $137,000 in full and final settlement. The case and its background should have at least raised alarm bells when in June 2003, the Arvizo family suddenly remembered significant instances of abuse by Michael against Gavin.

Yet most alarmingly, having suddenly remembered that Michael had repeatedly molested Gavin, the Arvizo family chose to report the matter not to the police but to lawyer Larry Feldman, the same lawyer who had handled the earlier Jordie Chandler case! Just as had happened a decade earlier, the youngster was seen by a psychiatrist who listened to the latest set of allegations against Michael Jackson and, as required to by law, reported them to the relevant authorities.

Armed with the new allegations, Michael's nemesis Tom Sneddon instigated a further and fuller investigation. The Arvizo family was interviewed at length and a list of charges was compiled. On 18 November 2003, while Michael was in Las Vegas to shoot a video for 'One More Chance', a new song on the compilation album *Number Ones*, more than 70 investigators armed with a search warrant (they also held an arrest warrant for Michael) descended on Neverland and undertook a thorough search of the estate. Two days later Michael flew into Santa Barbara airport and surrendered to the police, from where he was placed in handcuffs and driven to the local county jail. The television pictures of Michael being led away in handcuffs caused a furore around the world, not least since

Michael had voluntarily surrendered to the police and had shown no signs of attempting to escape or become violent. Michael would later charge that he had been physically abused during the arrest procedure, but the police released CCTV footage from inside the jail that showed Michael had been well treated.

Eventually, on 18 December Michael was charged with seven counts of child molestation and two counts of administering an intoxicating agent in order to commit that felony, all of the charges occurring between February and March 2003 and against the same boy. The charge further stated that on seven occasions Michael had 'wilfully, unlawfully and lewdly committed a lewd and lascivious act upon, and with, the boy's body and certain parts and members thereof, with the intent of arousing, appealing to and gratifying the lust, passions and sexual desires'. It was further charged that on two occasions, Michael 'had administered to the boy an intoxicating agent with intent thereby to enable and assist himself to carry out the previously mentioned act.' Bail was ultimately set at $3 million. A request to have the amount reduced (Phil Spector's bail on his murder charge had only been set at $1 million) was opposed by the prosecutor on the grounds that Michael might attempt to flee the country.

Michael was arraigned on 16 January 2004, turning up at court some 20 minutes late for which he was duly admonished by Judge Rodney Melville. After hearing the charges, Michael entered a plea of 'Not Guilty' and after leaving the court, delighted the hundreds of fans who had turned up to back him by jumping on to the roof of a parked SUV and doing a dance!

The legal machinations continued for several months, as both prosecution and defence gathered their evidence and compiled their witnesses. Judge Melville stated that he wished to have the trial begin by the end of 2004, with both sides agreeing that this was possible. In the event, jury selection did not take place until January 2005 and took less than a month, although it would have been completed earlier but for a bout of flu that hospitalised Michael for a few days. The final papers submitted to the court showed that the prosecution intended calling 91 witnesses, while the defence would call 50, although these figures were less than originally intended.

The opening statements were made on 28 February 2005 and the final verdict was eventually delivered on 13 June 2005. In between time, the very character of Michael Jackson was dragged through the mud, with all manner of charges and allegations being made in court. Yet as strong as the evidence against him seemed, several of the prosecution witnesses were just not believable. Two of them, Gavin and Janet Arvizo, admitted to having lied under oath in previous unrelated court cases. Additionally, Janet Arvizo chose to invoke the Fifth Amendment regarding welfare fraud she had committed. With the credibility of the main witnesses questioned, several of the other prosecution witnesses came under similar scrutiny – there were several obviously disgruntled ex-employees whose reliability would also be questioned.

Conversely, the witnesses called to testify on Michael's behalf included stellar names from the field of entertainment. When the prosecution tried to show alleged previous sexual behaviour of a similar nature, Macaulay Culkin was one of the witnesses who testified there had never been any sexual contact between him and Michael Jackson. Jordie Chandler made sure he was not called; he left the country in order to avoid testifying!

The almost four months of court appearances proved to be a trial in more ways than one for Michael. While his family, including his mother and father (with whom he had effectively become reconciled) attended each and every day in order to give their emotional support, at times he needed physical support just to get through the doors. He turned up apparently wearing his pyjamas underneath his jacket on one day, appeared to be close to collapse on others and looked frail and weary throughout the whole process. He turned up one day late enough to be under threat of losing his bail bond, such was the pressure on him. One can but imagine what was going through his mind as his detractors detailed a seemingly endless list of accusations, laying bare his innermost secrets in an attempt to further tarnish his name.

The closing arguments were held on 2 and 3 of June, after which the jury retired to consider their verdicts. They returned to court on 13 June and returned a Not Guilty verdict on all charges. As each of the charges and verdicts were read aloud by clerk Lorna Frye, a woman in the crowd outside released a white dove into the California air.

CHAPTER FOURTEEN
THIS IS IT!

Michael Jackson may have walked out of the court a free man but he was in many ways a broken man. The investigation and court case had taken some 574 days, during which time his recording career had stalled, his already fragile finances had taken a considerable blow (court papers revealed that Michael was spending some $35 million a year against an admitted income of just $11 to $12 million and was close to bankruptcy), and even ex-wife Debbie Rowe had turned against him. Having gone to court in 2001 to have her parental rights terminated, she went back in 2004 to have the decision reversed. According to papers she submitted to the court, she was concerned that the children were being exposed to the teachings of the Nation of Islam, an organisation that had become firmly entrenched in the Jackson camp.

Michael's involvement with the Nation of Islam had been something of a surprise. Initially, the organisation had supplied security for Michael, although later would come accusations that they had virtually taken over his life, deciding what he did and when and for whom. In papers submitted to the court in support of her claim, it was stated 'because she is Jewish, Deborah feared the children might be mistreated if Michael continued the association.' Debbie would eventually get joint custody of Prince Michael and Paris.

The main result of the court case was that Michael's earning power was massively reduced. No longer a major priority at Sony, and with the rights to his repertoire a long way off reverting, Michael could do little but sit and watch as the label released a succession of albums over the next few years. Some, such as *Number Ones*, he actively collaborated with. The success of The Beatles' *1* album, a collection of their UK and US number one hit singles that had sold some 31 million copies, made it the second most successful compilation album of all time. The Eagles' *Greatest Hits 1971-1975* is the only album to have sold more copies. This had prompted several of the recording world's biggest names, both living and dead, to follow suit, with Elvis Presley's *Elv1s* going on to sell some nine million copies worldwide.

Michael had offered to add a new song, 'One More Chance', to the album, and was filming a video for it when the molestation accusations first surfaced. With the subsequent arrest and charges, the chances of the album doing the same kind of business in the US were extremely slim. When finally released in November 2003, it barely sold a million copies in the US and peaked at #13 on the charts. In the UK, where Michael had always enjoyed healthy sales, it performed nearer to its true worth, topping the charts and going on to sell more than 1.5 million copies. Prior to Michael's death, the album had sold some six million copies worldwide, way off the expectations when the idea was first put together.

A year later, in December 2004, came *The Ultimate Collection* – a four CD compilation that barely made the Top 75 in the UK. In July 2005, Sony tried again with a double album entitled *The Essential Michael Jackson*, mixing material from both his Motown and Epic days. A number two hit in the UK, where it sold some 200,000 copies in five months, it was to be the album that registered the biggest increase in sales following Michael's death, shooting up the charts and eventually hitting the top. In the US, when originally released, the album limped in at #96 and sold under half a million copies, although it boosted its sales figures when Michael announced his live dates in March 2009 and performed even better following his death.

In February 2008, with *Thriller* having reached its 25th anniversary, Sony put together a special edition of the album that featured the original nine tracks, the Vincent Price excerpt from the original session, one track ('For All Time') that had been recorded for the original album but omitted, and 2008 remixes and new vocal versions of the five of the original tracks from the album, featuring the likes of Will I Am (from Black Eyed Peas), Akon, Fergie (also from Black Eyed Peas) and Kanye West, plus a special DVD that included the original videos for 'Billie Jean', 'Beat It' and 'Thriller', and Michael's performance from the *Motown 25* television special. This album at least rekindled interest in an artist who had seemingly turned his back on his career at the time, selling some three million copies in 12 weeks around the world.

The success of *Thriller 25* prompted Sony to look at compiling an album for Michael's forthcoming 50th birthday, with fans worldwide voting on the tracks that would be included within each individual country (the one exception being in the United States, where the album was not released!). Thus 21 different versions of the album were released worldwide on dates ranging from 22 August through to 12 December, in countries as diverse as South Korea, Finland, New Zealand, Brazil, Turkey and Poland. In the UK a total of 65,000 people voted for their favourites – among 50 titles that were pooled – resulting in a 17 track edition being released on 25 August and hitting #3 on the charts. A month later a three-disc deluxe edition was released, the second disc containing a further 18 tracks and the third disc being given over to rarities and remixes.

As successful as the various compilations were, sales were never going to reach the same giddy heights achieved by such classics as *Off The Wall, Bad* or even *Dangerous*. Michael's finances therefore continued to take a battering. He effectively abandoned Neverland as a home following the police raid of November 2003, and eventually closed the property as a cost-cutting exercise in 2006.

With his earning potential curtailed, Michael took to borrowing money from a variety of sources, initially using his part ownership of the Sony/ATV Publishing company. Some $270 million was borrowed using this as security, but Michael would default on the repayments and a refinancing package moved the loans from Bank of America to Fortress Investments. Michael approached Sony to obtain further funds, with Sony putting forward a proposal that would see them advance him $300 million, enabling him to reduce the interest rate payable on his original borrowing. The payback for Sony was that they would have a future option to buy 50% of Michael's stake in their joint venture, thus reducing Michael's ownership of Sony/ATV to just 25%. Michael would agree to the deal, although the specific financial details were not made public.

Even with 25% of the company, the value of Michael's stake continued to grow. In 2007 Sony bought Famous Music from Viacom for a reported $370 million, giving them immediate access to thousands of songs from artists as diverse as Eminem, Duke Ellington, Linda Perry and innumerable hit songs from films including 'Moon River', 'Footloose' and 'Take My Breath Away'. According to Forbes, the annual income to Michael from these holdings amounted to some $75 million. The problem was that according to other sources, Michael was routinely spending more than this!

In October 2007 it was announced that foreclosure proceedings had begun on Neverland, although Michael's people were quick to counter that the property was merely being re-financed. In February 2008, Financial Title Company informed Michael that unless he paid off nearly $25 million by the following month, a public auction would see the land, buildings, art and the assorted fixtures and fittings that Michael had accumulated sold off. Michael managed to stave off this, making a private agreement with Fortress Investment to save his continued ownership of the property. In 2008 another investment company, Colony Capital LLC, purchased the loan, with Michael expressing his satisfaction with the new deal. 'I am pleased with recent developments involving Neverland Ranch and I am in discussions with Colony and Tom Barrack [the owner of Colony] with regard to the Ranch and other matters that would allow me to focus on the future.'

Part of the deal saw Michael retain ownership of an unspecified proportion of the ranch in return for a payment of $35 million, money Michael was in dire need in order to pay other pressing debts.

Indeed, given the amount of money Michael had earned during the course of his career, there were plenty who were wondering where it had all gone. While he was known for his outrageous spending habits, surely there had to be something left in the pot? His finances may well take many years to finally unravel, but it would be fair to say that a considerable portion had gone on numerous legal battles. It was estimated, a few years into the millennium, that Michael had been involved in some 1,500 legal cases during the course of his career! Of course, not all of these ended in defeat and not all of them had cost him the kind of money he had had to hand over to Jordie Chandler, but the expense of retaining lawyers to help him handle all of the battles would have made a significant dent into his fortune.

Michael's never-ending need for money to keep himself afloat saw him rent properties around the world as he flitted from one country to another in search of somewhere to call home on a more permanent basis. He tried obtaining loans under a number of different aliases (usually unsuccessfully, since his credit rating was so low) and accepted advances to record a new album without ever entering a studio and subsequently was sued for its return.

While his earning potential from new and old material was drastically reduced, there was one surefire way of banking the kind of money he had enjoyed earlier on during his career: touring. There had been many offers since the 1997 world tour to return to the stage and Michael must surely had looked on enviously at the kind of money lesser names had earned from touring during the new century. For Michael even to contemplate going back on the road, the money would have to be more than worth it: it would have to be almost a record breaking offer. Enter AEG Live.

As both a promoter and owner of concert venues around the world, AEG Live had already been responsible for some of the biggest concerts in the world. The thought

of luring Michael Jackson back on the road for a series
of concerts was one that AEG Live president and chief
executive Randy Phillips felt was worth pursuing and, not
for the first time, Michael Jackson found he was under
almost constant pressure to deliver a 'yes' reply.

On 5 March 2009 a press conference was called at the
O2 Arena in London. The world knew some of what was
coming, enough to attract 7,000 fans and 350 reporters
to see what was in store on the day. Hours before the
conference began, a series of posters went up around
London announcing effectively a residency at the venue.
A lengthy commercial, seen by some 11 million people,
also aired the same evening. The plans were certainly
grand: Michael had agreed to do a ten-date residency
commencing on 8 July 2009. At the press conference,
Michael said 'I just wanted to say that these will be my
final shows ... performances in London. When I say this
is it, I mean this is it. I'll be performing the songs my fans
want to hear. This is it, this is really it, this is the final
curtain call.'

Ticketing arrangements for the shows required the
public to register their interest online, a request that caused
the system to crash as some 16,000 applications were
received *per second*. In all, some one million applications
for the tickets were received from fans in over 200
countries, resulting in the original ten dates being extended
to 31 and then 50 dates at the O2 between 8 July 2009 and
6 March 2010.

According to Randy Phillips, extra dates could have
been added to this tally and still sold, but Michael
apparently had other career plans that meant 50 dates was
the maximum that could be accommodated at the time.
This, however, does not entirely match with what became

known following the singer's death: the dancers that were contracted to the show signed contracts for two years, not one, and Phillips himself admitted that there was a three-and-a-half year contract in place between AEG Live and Michael Jackson.

At the beginning of May 2009, thousands of dancers flew into Los Angeles to audition at the Staples Center. Michael himself helped select the 12 who would eventually sign up for one of the grandest shows on earth; a total of some £13 million was being spent on producing the concerts, which were to feature between 18 and 22 songs and 22 different stage sets.

Yet while the dancers were being selected and the stage sets designed, Michael himself showed little sign of getting ready for what were the most eagerly awaited concert dates in more than a decade. He began his preparations late, working with former 'Hulk' actor Lou Ferrigno in order to build up his body strength, and privately stated to friends that he thought the shows were too much for a man of his age to contemplate. Eventually Michael persuaded AEG Live to agree with him: on 20 May an announcement was made that the opening dates had been moved back five days and that the new schedule would commence with 27 shows from 13 July to 29 September. There would then be a three-month break, followed by 23 shows between 7 January and 6 March 2010. Those who had seats for the original six dates were among the most vociferous in announcing their disappointment at this turn of events.

The following month Michael's legal problems raised their ugly head again, with concert promoter Allgood Entertainment suing Michael for some $40 million and claiming that they had an agreement with the singer for a $30 million reunion concert with his brothers and sister Janet. According to Allgood, the contractual agreement they had with Michael prevented him from performing elsewhere before the reunion concert or for three months after it – the 50 date residency at the O2 was therefore in breach of this contract and that AEG Live were aware of the restrictions and had used their dominance in the industry to get Michael to agree to the O2 dates.

The validity of this alleged contract had not been established as the month progressed. Michael continued to rehearse and, while he may have been late starting, he was certainly back to something approaching his best as the July dates got closer. While it was invariably claimed, especially in the immediate aftermath of his death, that his body was not up to the task of performing such a residency, footage released by AEG Live of a rehearsal filmed some two days before his death showed that Michael looked more than capable of entertaining his fans and confounding his critics.

It is doubtful whether any celebrity's death has been the subject of such intense media coverage, speculation, rumour and counter rumour as that which has followed the untimely death of Michael Jackson. Indeed, it may be some considerable time – if ever – before the full story can confidently be told, as the background story continues to emerge, and as more and more information comes into the public domain.

What is known at the time of writing is that at some time on 25 June Michael suffered a cardiac arrest at his rented house in Holmby Hills, was treated by paramedics at the scene and was pronounced dead at the Ronald Reagan UCLA Medical Center some two hours later.

The evening before Michael had arrived at the Staples

Center at 6.30 in the evening for rehearsals and had complained of laryngitis, which put back the rehearsal's start to 9.00pm. According to those present, rehearsals lasted for some three hours and Michael had looked in fine form, before heading back to the house in Carolwood Drive. According to Michael's physician Conrad Murray he [Murray] spent the night at the house, at the singer's request. The following morning, when Michael had not appeared out if his bedroom, Dr Murray went into the room and found that Michael was lying in the bed and not breathing. He felt for a pulse and observed only a weak pulse in the femoral artery – and also that the body was still warm. Murray attempted CPR for some five to ten minutes, without success, and then felt he should call for help. He did not use his own mobile phone as he said he did not know the exact address of the house, so instead called unsuccessfully for security and then ran downstairs and told the chef in the kitchen to get security and assistance up to the bedroom.

According to later reports, it was some 30 minutes before a 911 call was placed, 12-year-old Prince Michael was present during the CPR attempts, and the 911 call was only made after Michael's father Joseph had been informed by a security guard that his son was ill. As is apparently the norm in Los Angeles, various sections of the media routinely scan the airwaves for details, however sketchy, of requests for medical assistance and marry up the addresses given to those known to belong to or to be rented by celebrities. Thus, when paramedics left the house at Carolwood Drive, a horde of reporters and film crews had descended on the property to witness the ambulance leaving and driving to the UCLA Medical Center. Upon arrival at the UCLA Medical Center, a team of emergency physicians and cardiologists worked for over an hour, trying to resuscitate the stricken singer, before announcing his death at 2.26 pm.

The following day the body was moved to the LA Coroner's office in Boyle Heights, where a three-hour autopsy was performed. The brain was retained by the coroner and the rest of the body released to his family, who arranged for a second autopsy the following day (27 June). According to the investigator from the coroner's office there was no evidence of trauma or foul play, although the full toxicology tests would take four to six weeks to complete.

Even before the memorial service was held, stories about what had contributed to Michael's death were circulating throughout the media. According to sources close to the singer, there were serious concerns over his health. 'He wasn't eating, he wasn't sleeping and, when he did sleep, he had nightmares that he was going to be murdered. He was deeply worried that he was going to disappoint his fans. He even said something that made me briefly think he was suicidal. He said he thought he'd die before doing the London concerts. He said he was worried that he was going to end up like Elvis. He was always comparing himself to Elvis, but there was something in his tone that made me think that he wanted to die, he was tired of life. He gave up. His voice and dance moves weren't there any more. I think maybe he wanted to die rather than embarrass himself on stage.'

That would appear to be a rather fanciful assessment of Michael in the last few days and weeks leading up to his death, if only because there is one thing Michael would not have left behind knowingly: his three children.

Again, according to a barrage of stories that emerged,

Michael Jackson's problems stemmed from his drug abuse. While he acknowledged that he had become addicted to painkillers following the accident whilst filming the Pepsi commercial in 1984, there had been frequent attempts to battle the addiction, including therapy. Yet according to reports after his death, he had been given Deprivan intravenously (this drug is apparently only used *inside* hospitals and given to patients who are undergoing major surgery) as well as painkillers Demerol and Oxycodone as well as Xanax (an anxiolytic) and Zoloft (an anti-depressant), and he was also known to have used Prilosec, Vicodin, Paxil, Soma and Dilaudid. Police who searched his home also found several other drugs, some made out to Michael in his own name as well as several bottles that had no labels on whatsoever.

Since it may be months, and even years, before the full facts surrounding Michael's death are known, much of what has been reported can be safely attributed to wild speculation, malicious gossip and perhaps even outright lies for personal gain. Michael's will, which had been signed by him on 7 July 2002, was submitted to the Los Angeles County courthouse on 1 July by John Branca, who along with accountant John McClain was named as executor. The exact details of the will were not made public and all assets were handed immediately over to the Michael Jackson Family Trust. Associated Press reported that as of 2007, Michael had a net worth of $236.6 million, made up of $567.6 million in assets (including the Neverland Ranch and his share of the Sony/ATV Publishing Company) and debts of $331 million. Again, the full details and bequests in the will may take years to unravel, so complicated is the financial status of Michael Jackson.

Michael gave guardianship of his three children, Prince Michael, Paris and Prince Michael II to his mother Katherine, or if she was unable or unwilling, to Diana Ross. His former wife Debbie was intentionally omitted from the will, although she may benefit from the trust in the future.

There is no doubt that the major asset that Michael held was his stake in Sony/ATV Publishing. Estimates of the company's worth have varied between $1 billion and $4 billion, with the company itself remaining tight-lipped over whether it would attempt to buy out Michael's share from the estate. Michael's creditors may well have a major say in whether such a sale is forced through in order to realise cash with which to pay them back.

As with all major celebrity deaths, Michael's recorded catalogue undertook a major sales upswing, with *Number Ones* surging to the top of the UK album charts, to be replaced a week later by *The Essential Michael Jackson*, which was still at number one four weeks later. 'Man In The Mirror' bettered its earlier chart placing by reaching number two, and at one point Michael had no fewer than 22 titles in the Top 75.

On 7 July, at the Staples Center where he had been in rehearsal for the previous few months, the remaining Jackson family held a memorial service. A private family service was held at the Forest Lawn Hollywood Hills Cemetery before his brothers, all wearing a typical Michael Jackson jacket and a single glove, carried his casket into Staples Center, where 17,500 had gathered to pay homage. Tickets for the event had been allocated online, with those lucky enough to obtain one travelling to Los Angeles from all corners of the world. A worldwide television audience estimated at over a billion watched as Smokey Robinson began proceedings by reading messages of condolence from Diana Ross and Nelson Mandela. A gospel choir performed 'Soon And Very Soon' as the casket was brought into the auditorium and placed on the stage at the front of the hall. There followed performances by Mariah Carey and Trey Lorenz ('I'll Be There'), Lionel Richie ('Jesus Is Love'), Stevie Wonder ('I Can't Help It', the song Stevie had contributed to *Off The Wall*, an amended version of 'Never Dreamed You'd Leave In Summer' and 'They Won't Go When I Go'), Jennifer Hudson ('Will You Be There'), John Mayer ('Human Nature'), Michael's brother Jermaine, who sang his favourite song 'Smile', Usher ('Gone Too Soon'), Britain's Got Talent performer Shaheen Jafargholi ('Who's Lovin You') and an ensemble who sang 'We Are The World' and 'Heal The World'. Interspersed between the performances were speeches by Berry Gordy, Kobe Bryant, Magic Johnson, Brooke Shields, Martin Luther King III, Bernice King, Sheila Jackson-Lee, Smokey Robinson, Al Sharpton and eulogies from Jermaine and Marlon Jackson.

Also saying a few words was Michael's daughter Paris, who tearfully said 'I just want to say that ever since I was born, daddy has been the best father you could ever imagine...and I just want to say that I love him so much.'

The final resting place of Michael's body has not been revealed. It is known that the family would like to have the casket entombed in concrete (in order to prevent theft of the body, a fate which befell Charlie Chaplin) and eventually laid to rest at the Neverland Ranch, next to the train station that Michael used every day he was in residence in order to visit his private zoo. Unfortunately, since Californian law regulates where a body may be buried, the family may have to obtain special licence to carry out this plan.

There was much further speculation about other aspects of Michael Jackson's life and death in the weeks after his death. According to some reports, not one of the three children Prince Michael, Paris nor Prince Michael II are biologically his. Equally, Debbie Rowe was not the biological mother for Prince Michael or Paris, but a surrogate mother – and the father was her one time employer, Dr Arnold Klein. There was also a rumoured fourth child, Omar Bhatti, who was reportedly born after a one night stand in 1984 and conceived in a more conventional manner than the other three children.

Irrespective of what is true or untrue, right or wrong, real or imagined, there are several indisputable facts about Michael Jackson that are worth bearing in mind. It is doubtful whether there has been a performer who has been so universally admired and adored. There is certainly no other performer who has managed to cross over so many musical boundaries. There is no other entertainer who has done as much for or given so much to charity as Michael Jackson. Much of the outpouring of grief that followed his unexpected death was heartfelt, exceeding that which met the death's of Elvis Presley and John Lennon from the world of music and, yes, even Princess Diana from her own universe.

Perhaps most importantly, Michael showed us how to tear down colour boundaries. Elvis might have been a white singer who sounded black and enjoyed enormous success doing so, but Michael's achievement as a black performer appealing to all colours is probably a greater accomplishment.

Michael Jackson fascinated us as a bright eyed youngster singing 'I Want You Back' and 'ABC', captured our hearts as a teenager as he fronted 'Show You The Way To Go' and positively thrilled us as a young man with 'Billie Jean', 'Bad' and 'Earth Song'. The ticket demand that met his planned 2009 tour showed that he still had the ability to captivate, to excite and to enthral. No other entertainer has come close to matching the magic and mystery that was Michael Jackson.

Of his life, its twists and turns, joy and heartaches, perhaps Michael should have the final word. 'If you enter this world knowing you are loved and you leave this world knowing the same, then everything that happens in between can be dealt with.'

AWARDS

A full list of all the awards won by Michael Jackson would, quite literally, fill a second volume of this book. Below are some of the most significant awards which the singer has, to date, received. There may still be many more to come.

The awards are listed alphabetically, according to the body making the award.

AMERICAN CINEMA AWARDS
Jackson won the 'Entertainer of the Decade' award in 1990 from the American Cinema Awards.

THE AMERICAN MUSIC AWARDS
This is an annual awards ceremony created by Dick Clark in 1973. Picking up three awards in 1980, Jackson has collected 22 American Music Awards, including one for 'Artist of the Century'.

1980 Favourite Male Artist (Soul/R&B)
1980 Favourite Album (Soul/R&B): *Off the Wall*
1980 Favourite Single (Soul/R&B):
   'Don't Stop 'Til You Get Enough'
1981 Favourite Male Artist (Soul/R&B)
1981 Favourite Album (Soul/R&B): *Off the Wall*
1984 Award of Merit
1984 Favourite Male Artist (Pop/Rock)
1984 Favourite Male Artist (Soul/R&B)
1984 Favourite Album (Pop/Rock): *Thriller*

1884 Favourite Album (Soul/R&B): *Thriller*
1984 Favourite Single (Pop/Rock): 'Beat It'
1984 Favourite Video (Pop/Rock): 'Beat It'
1984 Favourite Video (Soul/R&B): 'Beat It'
1986 Award of Appreciation
1986 Song of the Year (with Lionel Richie)
　'We Are the World'
1988 Favourite Single (Soul/R&B): 'Bad'
1989 Award of Achievement
1993 International Artist Award
1993 Favourite Album (Pop/Rock): *Dangerous*
1993 Favourite Single (Soul/R&B): 'Remember the Time'
1996 Favourite Male Artist (Pop/Rock)
2002 Artist of the Century

AMERICAN VIDEO AWARDS
In 1984, Michael won two American Video awards;
Best Long Form Video and Best Home Video.

THE BILLBOARD MUSIC AWARDS
The Billboard Music Awards, sponsored by *Billboard*
magazine, were held annually in December until 2007.
Throughout his career, Michael won 40 *Billboard*-
related awards.

1972 Top Singles Artist of the Year Award
1972 Top Male Singles Artist of the Year Award
1983 Pop Artist of the Year Award
1983 Black Artist of the Year Award
1983 Pop Album Artist Award
1983 Pop Male Album Artist Award

1983 Pop Male Singles Artist Award
1983 Black Album Artist Award
1983 Black Singles Artist Award
1983 Pop Singles Artist Award
1983 Dance/Disco Artist Award
1983 Pop Album of the Year: *Thriller*
1983 Black Album: *Thriller*
1983 Dance/Disco 12": 'Beat It'
1983 Dance/Disco 12": 'Billie Jean'
1984 Top Album: *Thriller*
1988 Top Black Artist Award
1988 Blues & Soul Award
1988 Outstanding Artist of the Year Award
1988 Best Live Show Award
1989 #1 Album (Pop/R&B): *Bad*
1992 World Artist Award
1992 Commemoration for the 10th Anniversary of *Thriller*
1992 Hot 100 Singles Artist (Male) Award
1992 Hot R&B Singles Artist Award
1992 Hot Dance Music Club Play Artist Award
1992 Hot Dance Music Maxi-Single Sales Artist Award
1995 Special Hot 100 Award
1995 Video of the Year (Pop/Rock): 'Scream'

BILLBOARD MUSIC OF THE 80S POLL
1990 Black Artist of the Decade Award
1990 Black Single of the Decade: 'Billie Jean'
1990 Black Album of the Decade: *Thriller*
1990 Pop Album of the Decade: *Thriller*

BILLBOARD YEAR IN MUSIC SURVEY
1980 Top Black Artist Award
1980 Top Black Album: *Off the Wall*

BILLBOARD VIDEO AWARDS
1983 Best Performance by a Male Artist Award
1983 Best Overall Video: 'Beat It'
1983 Best Choreography: 'Beat It'
1983 Best Use Of Video To Enhance Artist's Song:
   'Beat It'
1983 Best Use Of Video To Enhance Artist's Image:
   'Beat It'

BMI URBAN AWARDS
Broadcast Music, Incorporated (BMI) is one of two major
United States performing rights organization, along with
ASCAP. It collects license fees on behalf of songwriters,
composers, and music publishers and distributes them as
royalties to members whose works have been performed.
BMI have presented Michael Jackson with four awards
during his career.

1990 1st Michael Jackson Award of Achievement
1993 Two of the Most Performed Songs of the Year:
   'Black or White', 'Remember the Time'
2003 BMI Urban Award: 'Butterflies'
2008 BMI Icon Award: The Jacksons

BRITISH PHONOGRAPHIC INDUSTRY AWARDS

This is the British record industry's trade association. They have given Jackson two awards over the years: the 1981 BPI Award for *Off the Wall* and the 1989 Video of the Year: 'Smooth Criminal'.

THE BRITS

Michael has won six awards at the BRIT Awards: Best International Male in 1984, 1988 and 1989, Best Album (for *Thriller*) in 1984, Best Video (for 'Smooth Criminal') in 1989 and an Artist of a Generation Award in 1996, the year he also performed at the awards ceremony.

CASHBOX AWARDS

Cash Box (or *Cashbox*) magazine was a weekly publication, produced from July 1942 to November 16, 1996. Cashbox awarded Michael Jackson 11 awards throughout his career.

1980 Soul Album of the Year: *Off the Wall*
1981 Soul Album of the Year: *Off the Wall*
1983 Number One Male Artist
1983 Top Black Male Artist
1983 Top Male Singles Artist
1983 Top Black Male Singles Artist
1983 Top Pop Album: *Thriller*
1983 Top Black Album: *Thriller*
1983 Top Pop Single: 'Billie Jean'
1983 Top Black Single: 'Billie Jean'
1989 Video Pioneer Award

GOLDEN GLOBE AWARDS

The Golden Globe Awards are presented annually by the Hollywood Foreign Press Association (HFPA) to recognize outstanding achievements in the entertainment industry. Michael Jackson received a Golden Globe for his song 'Ben', in 1972.

GRAMMY AWARDS

The Grammy Awards (originally called the Gramophone Awards)–or Grammys–are presented annually by the National Academy of Recording Arts and Sciences of the United States for outstanding achievements in the music industry. Michael has won 13 solo Grammy Awards during his career.

1979 Best Rhythm & Blues Vocal Performance:
'Don't Stop Till You Get Enough'
1983 Album of the Year in 1983: *Thriller*
1983 Record of the Year: 'Beat It'
1983 Best Rock Vocal Performance: 'Beat It'
1983 Best Pop Vocal Performance: 'Thriller'
1983 Best Rhythm & Blues Song
1983 Best Rhythm & Blues Vocal Performance:
'Billie Jean'
1983 Best Recording for Children: *E.T. The Extra-Terrestrial*
1983 Producer of the Year
1984 Best Video Album: *Making Michael Jackson's 'Thriller'*
1985 Song of the Year (with Lionel Richie)
for 'We Are The World'
1989 Best Music Video Short Form: 'Leave Me Alone'
1995 Best Music Video Short Form (with Janet Jackson):
'Scream'

GRAMMY HALL OF FAME

Two of Jackson's albums, *Off The Wall* and *Thriller,* were inducted into the Grammy Hall of Fame in 2008. The Jackson 5 song 'I Want You Back' was inducted in 1999.

HOLLYWOOD WALK OF FAME

Michael Jackson was the first celebrity to have two stars in the same category, one as a member of The Jacksons and another as a solo artist in 1984. Jackson's star is located between Highland Avenue and Orange Drive, along with the stars of Mickey Mouse, Barbara Streisand, Nicole Kidman, Harrison Ford, Halle Berry, Elton John and Anthony Hopkins.

MTV EUROPEAN MUSIC AWARDS

The MTV Europe Music Awards (EMA) were established in 1994 by MTV Networks Europe to celebrate the most popular music videos in Europe. Most of the awards are voted for by the viewers. Jackson won two EMA's in 1995, for 'Best Male Artist of the Year' and 'Best Male Performer.'

MTV VIDEO MUSIC AWARDS

The MTV Video Music Awards were established in 1984 by MTV to celebrate the top music videos of the year. In its debut show, the MTV Video Music Awards awarded Michael Jackson's 'Thriller' three awards. In all, Michael has won seven MTV Video Music Awards.

1984 Best Overall Performance Video: 'Thriller'
1984 Best Choreography: 'Thriller'
1984 Viewer's Choice Award: 'Thriller'
1989 Best Special Effects: 'Leave Me Alone'
1995 Best Choreography: 'Scream'
1995 Best Art Direction: 'Scream'
1995 Best Dance Video: 'Scream'

MTV VIDEO VANGUARD AWARDS

Jackson has received the MTV Video Vanguard Award twice. In 1991, the award was renamed as the 'Michael Jackson Video Vanguard Award'

1988 Video Vanguard Award
1989 The Greatest Video in the History of the World:
    'Thriller'

PRESIDENTIAL AWARDS

In 1984, Jackson was approached to donate 'Beat It' as backing music for a commercial on drunk driving. He agreed, and it was arranged for the singer to be awarded with an honour from the then President of the United States, Ronald Reagan. Prior to collecting the award, President Reagan sent Jackson a telegram, which read: 'Your deep faith in God and adherence to traditional values are an inspiration to all of us. You've gained quite a number of fans along the road since "I Want You Back" and Nancy and I are among them. Keep up the good work, Michael. We're very happy for you.'
The presentation took place on 14 May 1984, at the White

House. In April 1990, Jackson returned to the White House to meet President George W Bush, and while there President Bush recognised him as the 'Artist of the Decade'. On 1 May 1992, President Bush presented Jackson with an award acknowledging him as 'a point of light ambassador.'

ROCK AND ROLL HALL OF FAME

The Rock and Roll Hall of Fame is a museum located on the shores of Lake Erie in downtown Cleveland, Ohio, United States, dedicated to recording the history of some of the best-known and most influential artists, producers, and other people who have in some major way influenced the music industry.

Michael Jackson has been inducted into the Rock and Roll Hall of Fame twice: once as a member of The Jackson 5 in 1997, and subsequently as a solo artist in 2001.

UK MUSIC HALL OF FAME

Michael Jackson was inducted into the UK Music Hall of Fame in 2004, one of its first inductees.

DISCOGRAPHY

This Discography of Michael Jackson's singles and albums is complete up to the time of the singer's death. Chart re-entries after that date have not been included, as these will doubtless continue for years to come and cannot therefore be conclusively covered at this time. Catalogue numbers have also been omitted, as these vary from territory to territory.

JACKSON 5/JACKSONS SINGLES

TITLE	US	R&B	UK	COMPOSER	B-SIDE
BIG BOY	-	-	-	Ed Silver	You've Changed
WE DON'T HAVE TO BE OVER 21 (TO FALL IN LOVE)	-	-	-	Sherman Nesbary	Jam Session
I WANT YOU BACK	1	1	2	Freddie Perren/Fonce Mizell/Berry Gordy/Deke Richards	Who's Loving You
ABC	1	1	8	Freddie Perren/Fonce Mizell/Berry Gordy/Deke Richards	The Young Folks
THE LOVE YOU SAVE	1	1	7	Freddie Perren/Fonce Mizell/Berry Gordy/Deke Richards	I Found That Girl
I'LL BE THERE	1	1	4	Hal Davis/Berry Gordy/Willie Hutch/Bob West	One More Chance
SANTA CLAUS IS COMING TO TOWN	-	-	43	Haven Gillespie/J Fred Coots	Someday At Christmas/Christmas Won't Be The Same This Year
I SAW MOMMY KISSING SANTA CLAUS	-	-	-	Tommie Connor	Frosty The Snowman
MAMA'S PEARL	2	2	25	Freddie Perren/Fonce Mizell/Berry Gordy/Deke Richards	Darling Dear
NEVER CAN SAY GOODBYE	2	1	33	Clifton Davis	She's Good
MAYBE TOMORROW	20	3	-	Freddie Perren/Fonce Mizell/Berry Gordy/Deke Richards	I Will Find A Way
SUGAR DADDY	10	3	-	Freddie Perren/Fonce Mizell/Berry Gordy/Deke Richards	I'm So Happy
LITTLE BITTY PRETTY ONE	13	8	-	Bobby Day	If I Have To Move A Mountain
LOOKIN' THROUGH THE WINDOWS	16	5	9	Clifton Davis	Love Song
DOCTOR MY EYES	-	-	9	Jackson Browne	My Little Baby
CORNER OF THE SKY	18	9	-	Stephen Schwartz	To Know
HALLELUJAH DAY	28	10	20	Freddie Perren/Christine Yarian	You Made Me What I Am
SKYWRITER	-	-	25	Jerry Marcellino/Mel Larson	Ain't Nothing Like The Real Thing
GET IT TOGETHER	28	2	-	Berry Gordy/Hal Davis/Don Fletcher/Jerry Marcellino/Mel Larson	Touch
THE BOOGIE MAN	-	-	-	Deke Richards	Don't Let Your Baby Catch You
DANCING MACHINE	2	1	-	Hal Davis/Don Fletcher/Dean Parks	It's Too Late To Change The Time
WHATEVER YOU GOT I WANT	38	3	-	Mel Larson/Jerry Marcellino/Gene Marcellino	I Can't Quit Your Love
LIFE OF THE PARTY	-	-	-	Hal Davis/Tamy Smith/Clarence Drayton	Whatever You Got I Want
I AM LOVE (PART 1)	15	5	-	Mel Larson/Jerry Marcellino/Donald Fenceton/Roderick Rancifer	Part 2
FOREVER CAME TODAY	60	6	-	Brian Holland/Lamont Dozier/Eddie Holland	All I Do Is Think Of You

Title				Writers	B-side
ALL I DO IS THINK OF YOU	-	50	-	Eddie Holland/Michael Lovesmith	Forever Came Today
ENJOY YOURSELF	6	2	42	Kenny Gamble/Leon Huff	Style Of Life
SHOW YOU THE WAY TO GO	28	6	1	Kenny Gamble/Leon Huff	Blues Away
DREAMER	-	-	22	Kenny Gamble/Leon Huff	Good Times
GOIN' PLACES	52	8	26	Kenny Gamble/Leon Huff	Do What You Wanna
EVEN THOUGH YOU'VE GONE	-	-	3?	Kenny Gamble/Leon Huff	Different Kind Of Lady
DIFFERENT KIND OF LADY	-	-	-	Tito Jackson/Jermaine Jackson/Michael Jackson/Marlon Jackson/Randy Jackson	Find Me A Girl
MUSIC'S TAKING OVER	-	-	-	Gene McFadden/John Whitehead/Victor Carstarphen	Man Of War
FIND ME A GIRL	-	38	-	Kenny Gamble/Leon Huff	Different Kind Of Lady
BLAME IT ON THE BOOGIE	54	3	8	Mick Jackson/Dave Jackson/Elmar Krohn	Do What You Wanna
DESTINY	-	-	39	Tito Jackson/Jermaine Jackson/Michael Jackson/Marlon Jackson/Randy Jackson	That's What You Get
SHAKE YOUR BODY (DOWN TO THE GROUND)	7	3	4	Michael Jackson/Randy Jackson	All Night Dancin'
LOVELY ONE	12	2	29	Michael Jackson/Randy Jackson	Bless His Soul
HEARTBREAK HOTEL	22	2	44	Michael Jackson	Things I Do For You
CAN YOU FEEL IT	77	30	6	Michael Jackson/Jackie Jackson	Everybody
WALK RIGHT NOW	73	50	7	Michael Jackson/Jermaine Jackson/Randy Jackson	Your Ways
TIME WAITS FOR NO ONE	-	-	-	Jackie Jackson/Randy Jackson	Give It Up
THINGS I DO FOR YOU	-	-	-	Tito Jackson/Jermaine Jackson/Michael Jackson/Marlon Jackson/Randy Jackson	Your Ways
STATE OF SHOCK (with Mick Jagger)	3	4	14	Michael Jackson/Randy Jackson	Your Ways
TORTURE	17	12	26	Jackie Jackson/Kathy Wakefield	Instrumental
BODY	47	39	-	Marlon Jackson	Instrumental
WAIT	-	-	-	David Paich/Jackie Jackson	
TIME OUT FOR THE BURGLAR	-	88	-	Jackie Jackson/Randy Jackson/Bernard Edwards	
2300 JACKSON STREET	-	9	-	Teddy Riley/Gene Griffin/Jermaine Jackson/Randy Jackson/Tito Jackson/Jackie Jackson	
I WANT YOU BACK	-	-	8	Freddie Perren/Fonce Mizell/Berry Gordy/Deke Richards	
NOTHIN' (THAT COMPARES 2 U)	77	4	33	Kenneth Edmonds/Antonio Reid	Alright With Me
ART OF MADNESS	-	-	-	Jermaine Jackson/Michael Omartian/Bruce Sudano	

MICHAEL JACKSON SOLO SINGLES

TITLE	US	R&B	UK	COMPOSER	B-SIDE
GOT TO BE THERE	4	4	5	Elliot Willensky	Maria (You Were The Only One)
ROCKIN' ROBIN	2	2	3	Jimmie Thomas	Love Is Here And Now Your Gone
I WANT TO BE WHERE YOU ARE	16	2	-	Leon Ware/Arthur Ross	We've Got A Good Thing Going
AIN'T NO SUNSHINE	-	-	8	Bill Withers	I Wanna Be Where You Are
BEN	1	5	7	Don Black/Walter Scharf	You Can Cry On My Shoulder
WITH A CHILD'S HEART	50	23	-	Sylvia Moy/Henry Cosby/Vicki Basemore	Morning Glow
WE'RE ALMOST THERE	54	7	46	Brian Holland/Eddie Holland	We Got A Good Thing Going
JUST A LITTLE BIT OF YOU	23	4	-	Brian Holland/Eddie Holland	Dear Michael
MUSIC AND ME	-	-	-	Michael Cannon/Donald Fenceton/Mel Larson/Jerry Marcellino	Johnny Raven
EASE ON DOWN THE ROAD (with Diana Ross)	41	17	45	Charlie Smalls	Poppy Girls
YOU CAN'T WIN	81	42	-	Charlie Smalls	Part 2
DON'T STOP 'TIL YOU GET ENOUGH	1	1	3	Michael Jackson/Greg Philinganes	I Can't Help It
OFF THE WALL	10	5	7	Rod Temperton	Get On The Floor
ROCK WITH YOU	1	1	7	Rod Temperton	Working Day And Night
SHE'S OUT OF MY LIFE	10	43	3	Tom Bahler	Push Me Away
GIRLFRIEND	-	-	41	Paul McCartney	Bless His Soul
ONE DAY IN YOUR LIFE	55	42	1	Sam Brown III/Renee Armand	Take Me Back
THE GIRL IS MINE (with Paul McCartney)	2	1	8	Michael Jackson	Can't Get Outta The Rain
BILLIE JEAN	1	1	1	Michael Jackson	It's The Falling In Love
BEAT IT	1	1	3	Michael Jackson	Burn This Disco Out
WANNA BE STARTIN' SOMETHING	5	-	8	Michael Jackson	Rock With You
HAPPY (LOVE THEME FROM 'LADY SINGS THE BLUES')	-	-	52	Michel Legrand/William Robinson	We're Almost There
SAY SAY SAY (with Paul McCartney)	1	2	2	Paul McCartney/Michael Jackson	Ode To A Koala Bear
THRILLER	4	3	10	Rod Temperton	Things I Do For You
P.Y.T. (PRETTY YOUNG THING)	10	46	11	James Ingram/Quincy Jones	This Place Hotel
FAREWELL MY SUMMER LOVE	38	37	7	Kenny St Lewis	Call On Me
GIRL YOU'RE SO TOGETHER	-	-	33	Kenny St Lewis	Touch The One You Love
I JUST CAN'T STOP LOVING YOU	1	1	1	Michael Jackson	Baby Be Mine
BAD	1	1	3	Michael Jackson	I Can't Help It

Title				Writer	Note
THE WAY YOU MAKE ME FEEL	1	1	3	Michael Jackson	Instrumental
MAN IN THE MIRROR	1	1	21	Siedah Garrett/Glen Ballard	Instrumental
GET IT (with Stevie Wonder)	80	4	37	Stevie Wonder	Instrumental
DIRTY DIANA	1	5	4	Michael Jackson	Instrumental
ANOTHER PART OF ME	11	1	15	Michael Jackson	Instrumental
SMOOTH CRIMINAL	7	2	8	Michael Jackson	Instrumental
LEAVE ME ALONE	-	-	2	Michael Jackson	Instrumental
LIBERIAN GIRL	-	-	13	Michael Jackson	
BLACK OR WHITE	1	3	1	Michael Jackson/Bill Bottrell	Instrumental
BLACK OR WHITE REMIX	-	-	14	Michael Jackson/Bill Bottrell	Double A side
REMEMBER THE TIME/COME TOGETHER	3	1	3	Teddy Riley/Michael Jackson/Bernard Bell - John Lennon/Paul McCartney	
IN THE CLOSET	6	1	8	Michael Jackson/Teddy Riley	Radio edit
WHO IS IT	14	6	10	Michael Jackson	Oprah Winfrey intro
JAM	26	3	13	Rene Moore/Bruce Swedien/Michael Jackson/Teddy Riley	Rock With You (remix)
HEAL THE WORLD	27	62	2	Michael Jackson	She Drives Me Wild
GIVE IN TO ME	-	-	2	Michael Jackson/Bill Bottrell	
WILL YOU BE THERE	7	53	9	Michael Jackson	Instrumental
GONE TOO SOON	-	-	33	Lloyd Grossman/A Buz Kohan	
SCREAM	5	2	3	James Harris III/Terry Lewis/Michael Jackson/Janet Jackson	Childhood
SCREAM (REMIX)	-	-	43	James Harris III/Terry Lewis/Michael Jackson/Janet Jackson	
YOU ARE NOT ALONE	1	1	1	Robert Kelly	Scream Louder (remix)
EARTH SONG	-	-	1	Michael Jackson	
THEY DON'T CARE ABOUT US	30	10	4	Michael Jackson	Remix/Earth Song/Rock With You (remix)
WHY (with 3T)	112	72	2	Kenneth Edmonds	
STRANGER IN MOSCOW	91	50	4	Michael Jackson	Off The Wall (remix)
BLOOD ON THE DANCE FLOOR	42	24	1	Michael Jackson/Teddy Riley	Dangerous (edit)
HISTORY/GHOSTS	-	-	5	Michael Jackson/James Harris III/Terry Lewis - Michael Jackson	Double A side
YOU ROCK MY WORLD	10	13	2	Michael Jackson/Rodney Jerkins III/Fred Jerkins/Lashawn Daniels/Nora Payne	
CRY	-	-	25	Robert Kelly	
BUTTERFLIES	14	2	-	Marsha Ambrosius/Andre Harris	
HEAVEN CAN WAIT	-	72	-	Michael Jackson/Andreao Heard/Teddy Riley/Nate Smith/Teron Beal/Eritza Laues/Kenny Quiller	
ONE MORE CHANCE	83	40	5	Robert Kelly	
DON'T STOP 'TIL YOU GET ENOUGH	-	-	17	Michael Jackson/Greg Philinganes	
ROCK WITH YOU	-	-	15	Rod Temperton	
ONE MORE CHANCE	83	40	5	Robert Kelly	
THE GIRL IS MINE 2008 (with will.i.am)	-	-	32	Michael Jackson	
WANNA BE STARTIN' SOMETHING 2008 (with Akon)	81	-	69	Michael Jackson	